World War II

A PHOTOGRAPHIC HISTORY

World War II

A PHOTOGRAPHIC HISTORY

DAVID BOYLE

BARNES & NOBLE

NEW YORK

© 2006 by Rebo International b.v., Lisse, The Netherlands

This 1998 edition published by Barnes & Noble, Inc. by arrangement with
Rebo International b.v., Lisse, The Netherlands

Commissioned, edited and designed by Book Creation Services Ltd., London, Great Britain

Editor: Quentin Daniel
Designer: Bob Burroughs
Picture research: Mirco De Cet
Pre-press services: AdAm Studio, Prague, The Czech Republic

ISBN-13: 978-0-7607-1116-3
ISBN-10: 0-7607-1116-X

Printed and bound in Singapore.

20 19 1 8 17 16 15 14 13

Contents

THE CAMERA
AT WAR

In April 1940, an aerial photograph of the Nazi-held city of Bergen appeared in Britain's *Daily Mirror* newspaper. "We are bombing Bergen below," read the caption. "When you look at the picture, you are practically taking part in the raid – because you see exactly what the pilots saw from the cockpit."

It was a comparatively new experience for newspaper and magazine readers to see what pilots, soldiers and sailors had themselves witnessed. During World War II, the reality of combat was brought home to civilians day after day – not least because civilians were themselves often on the 'front line'.

For this was, after all, the first truly photographic war. Photographers of the Great War faced many difficulties: their camera equipment was unwieldy and their film had a relatively slow exposure time – hardly what was needed to capture action. Even when they came away with a powerful image, it was heavily censored by the military authorities, who distrusted

US Army photographers in action.

February 1945: US Marines landing on Iwo Jima, by Sergeant Neil Gillespie.

this still relatively new form of reportage. But a generation later the technology had vastly improved: action shots were now possible and cameras could be slipped into a pocket. Improved transport and communications also meant that pictures could be rapidly despatched to the influential new picture magazines – *Life* in the USA, *Picture Post* in Britain and *Signal* in Germany.

World War II photographers had many different motivations. In the build-up to the war, the Nazis had seized on the potential of photography as a propaganda weapon. Adolf Hitler, for example, was obsessed with creating the right kind of image of himself for posterity, banning photographs which showed him wearing glasses or leather shorts. With a sideswipe at Winston Churchill, he said "You can't be turned into a statue with a cigar in your mouth". Nazi propaganda chief Josef Goebbels had his own propaganda companies (PK) in every army unit, each one with over 100 vehicles and motorcycle messengers to take the film to the nearest air base. Every image taken by German military photographers was checked according to its likely effect on the war effort. The Russians had a

1941: A set-up photo of an Italian surrendering.

ABOVE: The Blitz spirit, London, November 1940. ABOVE RIGHT: British children shelter from an air raid, Kent 1940.

1941: A British army photo of troops rushing through the streets of Bardia, Libya.

30 April 1945: The Soviet flag is raised over the Reichstag, by Red Army photographer Yevgeni Khaldei.

similar policy. But being an official photographer for a totalitarian régime could be hazardous. German military photographers lacking ideological 'enthusiasm' were sent to the Russian front; Russian cameramen could face execution for producing 'defeatist' photographs.

In the democratic West, the attitude to official photographers was more tolerant. The general belief was that truth made the best propaganda – though of course subjects that might have a negative effect on morale, such as war dead, were deemed highly sensitive. The American army was keen to have photographers in its ranks; they were given four months' training, the rank of officers (*Life* photographers were colonels) and celebrity treatment. The British army, on the other hand, had smaller regard for cameramen: only 40 were taken on at the outbreak of hostilities – and they remained sergeants throughout the war.

Despite the technological advances, combat

Bert Hardy, *Picture Post* photographer.

Robert Capa of *Life* magazine.

photography was notoriously difficult. Few professionals had 'zoom' or telephoto lenses, and real action shots generally had to be taken close-up. Unsurprisingly, official photographers on both sides found themselves 'setting up' some shots behind the front line.

By contrast, the growing band of press photographers had more reason to protect their reputations: their names would appear below the published images. Some truly great photographers were active in World War II: Carl Mydans on the Russian-Finnish front, Bert Hardy in London during the Blitz, George Rodger in the North African desert and at Belsen, Ralph Morse in Guadalcanal, Eugene Smith in the Pacific, Yevgeni Khaldei with the Red Army in Berlin – the list goes on. By the end of the war, *Life* magazine had more photographers in the field than all the rest of the American press combined. Among their number was Robert Capa, whose photos of Omaha Beach on D-Day were unfortunately frazzled by a darkroom heater in London, leaving just 11 blurred shots.

The influence of press photographers grew as the war went on. In 1939, German restrictions meant that there were hardly any images of

ABOVE: 1945 – US troops in Panay, by Lt Robert Fields. RIGHT: 1943 – soldier in New Georgia, by Sgt J. Bushemi.

July 1941: London following an air raid, by Edward Worth.

the invasion of Poland. But the influence of Nazi censors began to wane as even they realized that photographs could be variously interpreted. For example, the famous image of St Paul's Cathedral in the smoke of the London Blitz, taken by Herbert Mason from the top of the *Daily Mail* building, was used by the British as a symbol of defiance and by the Germans as a symbol of London's destruction.

A huge quantity of war photographs were also taken by amateurs and bystanders. The Germans were so confident of final victory in Russia that they allowed their troops to carry their own Leicas; by the end of the war, half of all Allied servicemen were taking cameras into battle. Along with the press, such amateurs ensured that the reality of war appeared in print. *Life* fought a successful six-month battle to publish a GI's picture of three dead comrades on a Pacific beach; and it was a civilian, local newspaper photographer Yoshito Matsushige, who first captured the appalling effects of the atomic bomb on Hiroshima.

No matter what the circumstances in which they were taken, the photographs in this book graphically illustrate the many sides of the world's greatest conflict. They depict the extremes of human behaviour – the astonishing suffering and cruelty as well as the daily heroism and fortitude of hundreds of thousands of people. More directly than written records or dramatic interpretations, such images 'bear witness' – and through that, provide a warning from history.

EUROPE
THE WAR AGAINST FASCISM

THE ROAD TO WAR

The Seeds of Conflict

The origins of World War II lie in the immediate aftermath of the Great War. Britain, France and America had claimed victory from the slaughter of the Western Front, and were in a position to dictate terms to an impoverished, starving Germany. These terms were formulated in the Treaty of Versailles (1919). Universal conscription to the German army was forbidden; a vitally important part of the country, the Rhineland, was to be demilitarized; and the German state was forced to pay exacting reparations. Far from creating a contented peace, these measures bred acrimony and hatred. The German people saw the conditions of the treaty as effectively victors' vengeance; a popular catchphrase of the time spoke of Germany as 'heerlos, wehrlos, ehrlos' – 'disarmed, defenceless, dishonoured'.

Such grudges might gradually have been forgotten, had it not been for the Great Depression, which forced most Western industrialized

A poster celebrating Hitler's achievement in 'putting Germany back to work'.

The National Socialists go fund-raising against 'Hunger and Cold' in the streets of Berlin.

countries to suspend trade links with other countries. Germany, already weakened by its adherence to the terms of the Versailles treaty, was particularly badly hit. In the 1920s, unemployment rose to six million; the mark was drastically devalued; and international trade, such as it was, had to be carried out using the primitive system of barter.

As well as economic chaos, Germany was being torn apart by political strife. Russian revolutionary ideals had influenced the liberal German intelligensia, and communist-led strikers and police fought running battles on the streets of Berlin. The general public became disillusioned with the inability of the democratic government to control events, and to millions of Germans, the dream of strong, decisive rule soon became highly seductive.

There were plenty of extreme right-wing groups willing to make the dream a reality. The best organized of these were the National Socialists (Nazis), who gained notoriety in 1923 when one of their leaders, a slightly built, toothbrush-moustached ex-army corporal called Adolf Hitler, was jailed for a coup attempt in Munich.

In prison, Hitler set down his political credo in a book, *Mein Kampf* (*My Struggle*). On his release, he immediately set about establishing per-

Soup-kitchens are set up in the streets of Berlin for victim of the Great Depression.

The mid-1920s: National Socialists recruiting in Munich.

January 1933: Hitler celebrates becoming Reichschancellor.

The new Reichschancellor makes a typically fierce speech.

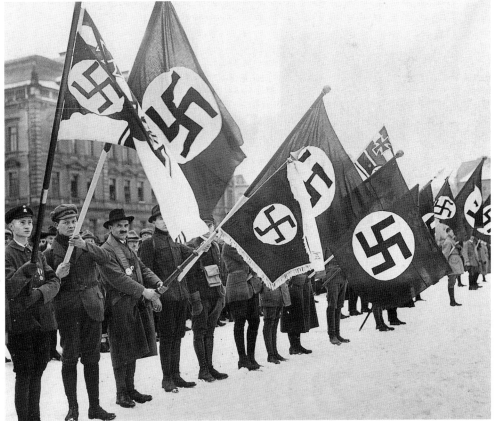

1933: Swastika-waving National Socialist workers in Munich.

The 1920s: Mussolini and his blackshirts in Rome.

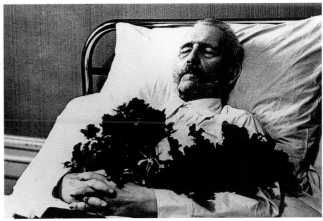

August 1934: Reichsführer Hindenburg dies.

sonal control over the Nazi party and fashioning a political platform that would attract a significant portion of the German electorate. He claimed to side with the underdog, the embittered, the put-upon – backing small shopkeepers against international banks and farmers against the 'moral degradation' of the cities. He railed against the terms of the Versailles treaty, and provided a convenient scapegoat for economic collapse – 'International Jewry'. He stressed the shared racial roots of 'true' Germans, and set out his concept of *Lebensraum* – 'living space'.

In January 1933, Adolf Hitler became Reichschancellor, given office by over a third of German voters. Within days of coming to power, he made a show of his 'strength' by declaring all meetings by the German communists illegal.

Four weeks later, on 27 February, the German parliament building, the Reichstag, caught fire, and Hitler used the blaze as an excuse to clamp down on his enemies. His uniformed brown-shirts were called out in force, and many communists were arrested that same night. Four of these were 'tried' and executed. The general election that followed gave Hitler and the Nazis complete control.

Stories about the Nazi attitude to the Jews were already circulating in Europe, but the true nature of the new German government only became apparent after Hitler purged his own party in the summer of 1934. Over 1000 perceived opponents and rivals for power

ABOVE: Mussolini enters Addis Ababa, May 1936.
FAR LEFT: The Reichstag fire of 27 February 1933.

The Führer with a favourite – Rudolf Hess.

Mid-1930s: Hitler signs autographs for members of the Hitler Youth.

were shot. When the brownshirt (SA) leader Ernst Röhm was arrested by Hitler in person, the shockwaves were felt by fascist parties the length and breadth of Europe.

At the end of the year, having been completely senile for some months, the German head-of-state Marshal Hindenburg died and Hitler adopted the title Reichsführer.

In the first years of his leadership, Hitler extended his control over every aspect of German life. All political parties were disbanded. The trade unions were replaced by a state-run Labour Front. The limited self-government of German provinces was abolished, and the Nazi party and German state declared one and the same. Hitler also made changes in the army: German soldiers had to take an oath in which they promised "unconditional obedience to Adolf Hitler, leader of the Reich and People".

Those few institutions that threatened to defy him, such as the Church, were rigorously controlled. "This is the last time a German court is going to declare someone innocent whom I have declared guilty," said Hitler, when the protestant theologian Martin Niemoeller was acquitted of subversion.

In Nazi-run Germany, opposition to Hitler had to be a secretive business – a thing of whispers and glances. For anti-Nazis had a great deal to fear. A joke about the Führer might lead to denunciation and arrest – and spies were everywhere. People were encouraged to keep watch over their neighbours on grounds of patriotism, and children were rewarded for informing on their parents. The first concentration camps were set up for 'idlers', 'sub-

SA leader Ernst Röhm.

A Nazi parade through the streets of Berlin.

Italian fascists on a tour of Germany.

Heinrich Himmler, head of the SS.

Julius Streicher, editor of *Der Sturmer.*

versives' and, under the Nuremberg decrees of 1935, Jews. Dissidents began to disappear, never to be heard of again. To swim against this tide required enormous courage – even foolhardiness.

Such was the iron grip that Hitler exerted over Germany in the mid-1930s that it is sometimes forgotten that the first truly fascist state was Italy. Benito Mussolini, known as 'Il Duce', had come to power in Italy as early as 1922. Though he was never to acquire the same degree of personal control as Hitler (the slogan 'Mussolini is always right', painted on walls all over Italy, may have been a sign of desperation), he did set in place the prototypical fascist state apparatus: a vast, centralized bureaucracy using secret police and informers as its instruments.

Mussolini also had imperial ambitions. He dreamed of creating a modern Roman Empire in the Mediterranean, with himself as Caesar. To this end, he sent his armies to Libya and Abyssinia where glorious military triumphs were recorded against handfuls of ill-equipped desert tribesmen. Hitler took note of his example – though his ambitions were more far-reaching.

Other European countries also had fascist movements and, by 1934, these were on the march. The right was particularly vociferous in France,

Streicher at the head of a brownshirt parade in Munich.

where rioting ex-servicemen forced the government out of office. In Austria, the socialist party was suppressed after days of armed resistance and Chancellor Engelbert Dollfuss was assassinated by the Nazis in July that year – a preliminary to the *Anschluss*, Hitler's forced union of Austria and Germany in 1938. In Spain, there was mounting fascist opposition to the leftist Republican government.

The Western democracies watched these events as though in a state of paralysis. Non-intervention was the watchword of the day, so few were surprised when the international rule of law, so idealistically created by the post-war allies to avoid further large-scale conflict, began to unravel. By the mid-1930s, the League of Nations had already begun to lose its influence and status. Japan took no notice of its protests in 1931 when its troops marched into Manchuria; Mussolini ignored its sanctions when he occupied Abyssinia in 1936. Hitler quit the League in 1933. His remilitarization of the Rhineland in 1936 raised scarcely a whimper.

By the late 1930s, the scales had been tipped still further towards war by the mutual suspicion of those nations which could guarantee peace. In the Soviet Union, Josef Stalin believed the capitalist powers would try to unite to bring down his régime. He was more prepared to counte-

BELOW: German troops enter the Rhineland, 1936.
OPPOSITE: Hitler passes in triumph through Vienna, 1938.

nance the fascist Hitler, in whose rule he perhaps recognized some distorted mirror image of his own tyranny. This perverse understanding was to lead to the Ribbentrop-Molotov pact of 1939, by which Poland and the Baltic states were cut up like a cake to be shared between the Reich and Soviet Russia.

The Western nations, on the other hand, regarded Hitler as a bulwark against communism in the East, and were prepared to turn a blind eye to his excesses. In the same way, Mussolini was seen as having saved Italy from bolshevism. The fascists were seen as a necessary and – it was hoped – passing evil.

There was another factor that Hitler was able to exploit. The prospect of another war aroused intense revulsion in British and French society, both still reeling from the carnage of the Western Front. Politicians fought shy of the question of rearmament; it was seen as electoral suicide. Army and navy budgets were cut, recruiting was suspended, innovation was discouraged – complacency reigned. Meanwhile, Hitler had embarked on a massive programme of rearmament, forging Germany into a weapon of war that he believed would one day – and sooner rather than later – conquer Europe.

ARMING FOR ARMAGEDDON

The Weapons' Build-up

"**P**ropaganda, propaganda, propaganda – all that matters is propaganda," said Hitler on the night of his failed coup attempt in 1923. Though he knew they were sick of economic, social and political chaos, even into the mid-1930s Hitler continued to doubt whether the German people were ready for another war. One of the chief ends of Nazi propaganda was to prepare them for it. When Hitler came to power in 1933, the Nazi message was that, though Germany remained the victim of injustice, it was getting stronger. The martial virtues and self-sacrifice of the *Volk*, the mythologized German people, were celebrated in mass rallies at Nuremberg and elsewhere, but Hitler's propaganda chief Josef Goebbels made sure that the word 'war' was used as little as possible. No reference to conflict was made by the Nazi leaders even during the Munich crisis of 1938.

ABOVE: Panzers on military exercises. OPPOSITE: Hitler salutes adoring crowds in Munich.

Fighters on the production line.

Working on cockpit circuitry.

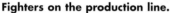

Mk1 Panzers practise column advance.

Of course, propaganda was not enough. German military power also had to be rebuilt. Conscription was reintroduced in 1935 – again contrary to the terms of Versailles – and the same year the creation of the *Luftwaffe*, or air force, was officially announced. The build-up of this was put under the control of Hermann Goering, also Hitler's chosen successor. Goering, though vain, fat and addicted to morphine, had been a pilot in the Great War and was a capable organizer. He agreed with Hitler that air power would be a crucial factor in any future war: both had seen how Mussolini's air force had terrified the desert tribesmen in Libya and Abyssinia. Aircraft soon began to roll off the Messerschmitt and Heinkel production lines at a tremendous rate, and German pilots went into action in support of the Spanish fascist General Francisco Franco over Barcelona and Guernica.

ABOVE: A panzer group practises signalling techniques. BELOW: General Rommel and aides check maps on manoeuvres.

Hitler's propaganda chief Josef Goebbels.

Luftwaffe chief Hermann Goering.

Flag-bearers at a Nuremberg rally.

Poster for the Berlin Olympics.

Hitler was fortunate, too, in the advice he received from some of the more forward-looking generals in the *Wehrmacht*, or German army. They spoke of the effect that tanks would have on the modern battlefield, and particularly admired a book on the subject written by a French colonel, Charles de Gaulle. Used in conjunction with airstrikes, panzer divisions could smash enemy resistance and spearhead the advance of infantry; great distances could be covered in a single day in a strategy formulated as 'lightning war' – *Blitzkrieg*.

At the same time, Hitler set about rebuilding the German navy, largely scrapped at the end of the Great War. But he had no desire to antagonize the British, still possessors of one of the world's largest fleets, before it was absolutely necessary. In June 1935, therefore, he signed the Anglo-German Naval Agreement, by which he was permitted to build a fleet a third the size of the Royal Navy. But he lied about the numbers of ships already under construction, and the British saw no threat in his apparently innocent proposal to build more U-boats – later to become the scourge of the North Atlantic.

In the event, his ruse was merely a delaying tactic. A year later, by abandoning the arms limitation Treaty of Locarno, Hitler gave up all

Hitler acknowledges the crowd at the Olympics.

Hitler at Nuremberg – the centre of Nazi pageantry.

The Führer congratulates brownshirts at a pre-war rally.

Nazi leaders salute SA men in Nuremburg.

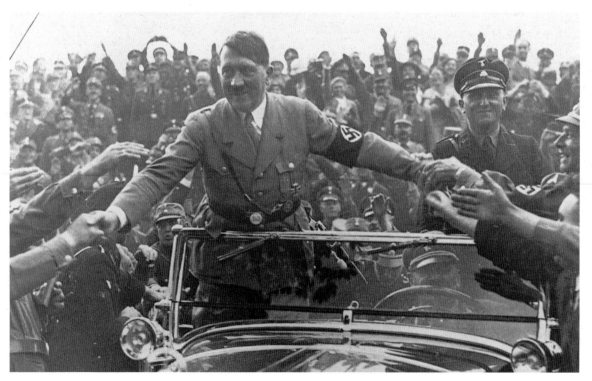

Hitler's popularity grows.

pretence of abiding by weapons' quotas. Britain and France received a nasty shock; they made frantic efforts to set the rusty wheels of rearmament turning again. However, the French were hampered by an old-fashioned industrial system, the British by the effects of the Depression and political opposition.

The Western democracies were also completely outmanoeuvered by Hitler's diplomatic offensive. In 1936 he signed the Anti-Comintern Pact with Japan, while in May 1939 he concluded a defence agreement with Mussolini, the so-called 'Pact of Steel'. Meanwhile, his foreign minister Joachim von Ribbentrop had begun secret negotiations with the Nazis' declared arch-enemy, Josef Stalin.

SS standard-bearers – a deliberate echo of the Roman legions.

THE SHAME OF APPEASEMENT

Attempts to Placate Hitler Fail

"The history of all times – Roman Empire, British Empire – has proved that every space expansion can be effected only by breaking resistance and taking risks," wrote Hitler in *Mein Kampf*, explaining Germany's need for *Lebensraum*. "Neither in former times nor today," he went on ominously, "has space been found without an owner". Germany's space problem would have to be solved by 1945, he claimed; after that there would be a food crisis.

Reading Hitler should have put his contemporaries in no doubt about his aims; it was certainly clear his ambitions went beyond regaining territory lost in the Treaty of Versailles. But the British and French leaders, for the political and psychological reasons already discussed, were prepared to ignore his encroachments on neighbouring territory. Their policy of appeasement was designed to satisfy Hitler's appetite for land – which they did not believe was insatiable – as well as the overwhelming desire for peace felt by their populations. The remilitarization of the Rhineland and the Nazi aid sent to General Franco were held up as warnings by French and British leftists and conservatives alike. But most held stubbornly to the view that Hitler was a relatively rational being with more or less legitimate aims; any 'excessive' aggression, they argued, could be discouraged with a demonstration of unity and even a show of strength.

But Britain and France were neither united nor willing to warn Hitler explicitly. On the contrary, their message to him was confused and weak. In November 1937, the Nazis were much encouraged by a visit from the senior British politician Lord Halifax, who allowed Hitler to believe that Britain would give him a free hand in eastern Europe as long as there were "no far-reaching disturbances". Hitler had already been convinced that the British upper classes would not fight by the controversial motion carried in the debating forum of Oxford University, the Oxford Union, that students would 'not fight for King and Country'.

A few months later, the British foreign secretary Anthony Eden resigned over his government's approach to Hitler. "Go home and take an aspirin," he was told by prime minister Neville Chamberlain, and Halifax was appointed in his place.

"Peace in our time" – Chamberlain returns with the Munich Agreement.

In March 1938, when Hitler annexed Austria, he told his own military leaders that lack of opposition to it was proof of western spinelessness. Neither Britain or France, he indicated, would have the stomach to defend a 'third country' if he attacked it. He meant Czechoslovakia, and he was right.

The so-called Munich Crisis of September 1938 was the biggest test yet of the appeasement policy. Czechoslovakia, a democracy, was almost entirely surrounded by Germany and inhabited by over three million

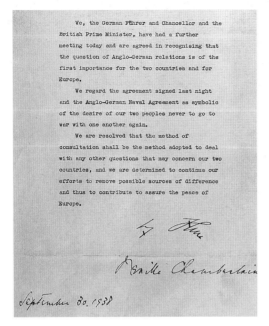

We, the German Führer and Chancellor and the British Prime Minister, have had a further meeting today and are agreed in recognising that the question of Anglo-German relations is of the first importance for the two countries and for Europe.

We regard the agreement signed last night and the Anglo-German Naval Agreement as symbolic of the desire of our two peoples never to go to war with one another again.

We are resolved that the method of consultation shall be the method adopted to deal with any other questions that may concern our two countries, and we are determined to continue our efforts to remove possible sources of difference and thus to contribute to assure the peace of Europe.

September 30, 1938

The Munich agreement.

German-speakers. Hitler spoke of these Sudeten Germans as a persecuted minority; at some point, he declared in a series of ferocious speeches, the will of the German people would force him to 'intervene'.

"Tomorrow, Hitler may attack Czechoslovakia," French foreign minister Georges Bonnet told the British ambassador to Paris on 10 September. "If he does, France will mobilize at once. She will turn to you saying: 'We march: do you march with us?' What will be the answer of Great Britain?"

Britain's answer was muddled. An order was given for partial mobilization of the armed forces, but diplomatic criticism was muted. Then, on the 29 September, Chamberlain and the French prime minister Edouard Daladier flew to Munich and took the train to Hitler's mountain retreat at Berchtesgaden. Negotiations were chaotic, as the nominal go-between Mussolini crowded the leaders into a room filled with officials eating buffet food.

The fate of the Sudetenland was sealed shortly after midnight.

Chamberlain had been convinced of three things: that, for all their protestations, the French would not fight, that allowing Germany to

ABOVE: German troops stand to attention in Prague. OPPOSITE: A Czech woman's grief-stricken submission.

May 1939: the Pact of Steel.

occupy the Sudetenland would prevent whole-sale invasion of Czechoslovakia, and that he could rely on Hitler's word to go no further. Neither he nor Daladier consulted the Czechs.

With the stroke of a pen, a sizeable chunk of a sovereign European country had been ceded to a totalitarian power. Those German generals who might have been prepared to overthrow Hitler had Britain and France stood up to him, now lent him their wholehearted support. The Munich agreement also encouraged Hitler to believe that the sabre-rattling of partial mobilization had been a face-saving device to quiet opposition to appeasement within Britain. His main concern was that a large number of German tanks had broken down on the way into the Sudetenland.

When a shamefaced Daladier returned to Paris, he thought the crowds awaiting him would tear him to pieces; in fact they were delighted. Chamberlain also returned to a hero's welcome, waving a piece of paper which he announced meant "peace in our time". As late as March 1939 he was assuring friends that prospects for peace were better than ever. But events rapidly took a different course.

Von Ribbentrop returns from negotiations in Moscow.

On 12 March 1939, encouraged by the Nazis, the Slovaks declared independence from the Czech section of Czechoslovakia. Britain and France had guaranteed the independence of the rest of the country at the Munich agreement, but Chamberlain told the House of Commons that Slovakian independence cancelled this obligation. The elderly Czech president Emil Hacha travelled to Berlin, where he received such a verbal battering from Hitler that he fainted; reluctantly he signed the document pushed in front of him, placing "the fate of the Czech people into the hands of the Führer of the German Reich".

Three days later, German troops marched into Prague and the successful Czech arms industry, which then accounted for 10 per cent of the world market, lay in Hitler's hands.

March 1938: Hitler arrives in Vienna.

But the Führer was not content, turning his covetous gaze northwards. On 21 March, his troops annexed Lithuania, and Chamberlain was compelled to alter his foreign policy. Eight days later, the British prime minister offered Poland a promise of support against any threat to its independence.

Polish foreign minister Colonel Beck took the decision to accept

September 1938: Ribbentrop and Chamberlain pass through the guard of honour at Munich Airport.

The Nazi-Soviet pact takes shape – Hitler meets Molotov.

Chamberlain's offer, he said, "between two flicks of the ash" of his cigarette. He wanted to give Hitler a slap in the face for his demands for the return of Danzig.

It was just the diplomatic ammunition Hitler needed. Both Beck and Chamberlain had overrated the ability of Poland's antiquated armed forces to resist invasion. The British cabinet and the chiefs of staff also knew their promise would be impossible to keep without help from Russia – but only the French made any attempt to deal with Stalin. Besides, the Poles were adamant that not one Russian soldier would set foot on Polish soil; they were afraid that once the Red Army crossed the border, it would never leave – a fear justified by later events.

But the diplomatic paper-shuffling in the West was in some ways marginal to events where it mattered. Longing to extend his own sphere of influence westwards, and furious that the Western allies had snubbed his offer of intercession over Czechoslovakia, Stalin had ordered his new foreign minister Vyacheslav Molotov to negotiate a pact with the Germans by which Poland would be divided equally between the two totalitarian powers. To the horror of the world's peacemakers, von Ribbentrop flew to Moscow to sign the pact on 23 August.

Peace in Europe lasted just 10 more days.

THE AXIS INVASIONS

GERMAN AND ITALIAN ARMIES ON THE MARCH

BLITZKRIEG

Hitler's Panzers strike at Poland

There was no Nazi declaration of war, no warning and precious little mercy. At 4.45 am on 1 September 1939, Hitler's troops crossed the Polish border in a pitiless demonstration of 'lightning war'. First Stuka dive-bombers hit communication lines and military strongpoints; panzers and motorized units rumbled across the flat Polish countryside, meeting only weak resistance. An hour later, waves of German Heinkels and Dorniers were droning over Warsaw. In the devastating series of bombing raids that followed, the terrified populace was sent scurrying for cover and half the Polish air force was destroyed on the ground.

Later that day, almost as an afterthought, Hitler informed the Reichstag that Germans were being 'massacred' in Poland and urgent intervention was needed.

Across Western Europe, the attack was regarded as a grim inevitability. The French and British began to mobilize their forces, though at the

September 1939: Polish troops mobilize, with Vickers E light tanks.

Polenfeldzeng in Poland: German forces demonstrate the
effectiveness of 'lightning war'. But Hitler's resources
had been stretched to the limit.

same time Halifax and Bonnet accepted an offer of mediation from
Mussolini. In Britain, the evacuation of nearly two million women and
children from the cities began, as bombardment from the air was
thought imminent.

It was the British House of Commons which tipped the balance in
favour of war. By 2 September, it was clear to Chamberlain that unless he
honoured his symbolic commitment to Poland in some way, his government would collapse. The cabinet refused to leave the room until the
decision to issue an ultimatum had been taken.

The next day at 9 am, the British ambassador to Berlin delivered his
ultimatum, demanding an undertaking that German troops would be

withdrawn within two hours. This was not forthcoming. At 11.15, Chamberlain broadcast the announcement that war had therefore been declared. The French also issued an ultimatum and at 5.00 pm this too expired unanswered.

Poland was too distant for the Allies to intervene directly, but the RAF attacked the German naval base at Wilhelmshaven, sustaining heavy losses. The French army reinforced the Maginot Line; they relied on a conscript army which took 16 days to mobilize, so no attack could be mounted quickly. Meanwhile, the Poles were discovering their plans to march on Berlin had been premature. Their soldiers, though courageous, were hopelessly under-equipped and badly prepared. They possessed only two

SS Field police enter Danzig with an ADGZ armoured car.

motorized brigades and fought only one major battle, at the River Bzura, as part of their retreat to Warsaw.

There was worse news to come. On 17 September, the Soviets began their own invasion of Poland from the east – ostensibly to protect White Russians and Ukrainians. Only 737 Russians were to be killed in the campaign. By 5 October, all Polish forces had surrendered; over 900,000 soldiers were prisoners of the Germans and Russians, and only about 70,000 had escaped. Many thousands were shot by their captors. Civilians fared little better, as Hitler signed a secret amnesty releasing all SS men arrested by the regular army for brutality against civilians. In the following two years, a fifth of the population was murdered.

Meanwhile, the elected Polish government had been interned in Romania, and a government in exile had been set up in Paris.

There is evidence to suggest that, had the French attacked Germany at this point, they would have met with almost no resistance. Hitler had gambled all in the rapid drive through Poland – his supplies were exhausted. But the Allies were paralysed by indecision. They seemed to be waiting for a miracle – for Hitler to withdraw out of the goodness of his heart, having made his example.

The complete defeat of Poland led to a long period of apparent quiet which the American press dubbed the 'Phoney War'. Much was expect-

Front line troops push into the Polish capital of Warsaw.

Storming through the outskirts of Warsaw.

ed, but little happened. Hitler made a peace offer which was rejected by Britain and France in public but discussed as a real possibility in private. He also began preparations for the invasion of France. The war would be fought, he now told the German High Command explicitly, "to decide the domination of Europe".

In France, the government had decided on war despite major misgivings; the National Assembly was not even allowed a proper vote on the declaration. They were just asked to decide on whether to "fulfil treaty obligations". Opponents in the debate were silenced, while outside the Assembly, right-wing politicians and the Communist PCF urged the government to come to terms. PCF leader Maurice Thorez deserted from the army to Moscow, while one French fascist asked, "Do you want to die for Danzig?" The nation's morale plummeted.

In Britain, black-outs began and park railings were torn up to be melted down for steel. British ships began sailing in convoy. Food was rationed from January 1940.

It was at this point that Sir Winston Churchill, long a Conservative MP in the political 'wilderness', returned to the British cabinet as First Lord of the Admiralty.

A British Expeditionary Force of four divisions was despatched to France under the hereditary Irish peer Lord Gort, a hero of the Great

ABOVE: A German warship bombards the Polish fort of Westerplatte. BELOW: Polish P.23b bombers.

War and Britain's most senior general. It was stationed along the border with Belgium, under the French supreme commander Maurice Gamelin – a long and passionate opponent of the idea of motorized warfare. A wrangle began over the exact limits of Belgian neutrality.

French policy depended on the Belgians, because the whole basis of French defence, the Maginot Line, did not extend along the Belgian border (where the Kaiser's troops had entered France a generation before). Even along the French border with Germany, the Maginot Line was not continuous; nonetheless, it would remain a formidable obstacle to Hitler's armoured columns.

All was not completely quiet. The British were already losing shipping to the new German magnetic mines and, on 14 October, the battleship *Royal Oak* was torpedoed and sunk by U-47 in its war-time anchorage, Scapa Flow.

However, there was one Allied success. Three British cruisers cornered the German pocket battleship *Graf Spee* outside Montevideo and, at the Battle of the River Plate on 13 December, inflicted enough damage to force its captain to scuttle it.

December 1939: British cruisers near the River Plate.

The pocket battleship *Graf Spee* burning off Montevideo.

From the start of hostilities, British and French politicians deluded themselves that the Nazi régime was running out of resources. Though Hitler's supplies were stretched, they were not on the point of collapse – and they had reckoned without the Soviet Union. Stalin was taking his agreement with Hitler seriously, and oil and coal poured into Germany from the east. The Soviet leader was also consolidating his position in the Baltic. On 30 November, Red Army troops had invaded Finland, following a minor border incident.

Although they were encouraged by the initial success of Finnish resistance, the Allied governments agonized for months about whether to send an expedition to help them. Apart from the logistical difficulties involved, it would not only have meant war with Soviet Russia, but flouting the neutrality of Norway and Sweden. Then, on the 11 March 1940, just before the preliminary expedition could leave, the Finns finally accepted Soviet terms. In the aftermath of this débacle, Daladier was ousted as French prime minister and replaced by the much more bellicose Paul Reynaud.

Reynaud flew straight to London for a meeting of the Allied Supreme War Council, urging decisive action. There was a feeling, again, that Hitler had lost his direction. "Mister Hitler has missed the bus," pronounced Chamberlain on 4 April, as the Allies prepared to lay mines in Norwegian waters to cut the iron ore route into Germany.

He could not have been more mistaken. Mining definitely violated Norwegian neutrality and gave German forces the perfect excuse for invasion. An incident in February had tipped the balance in favour of the idea, when the British destroyer *Cossack* chased the German *Altmark* into a Norwegian fjord to rescue Allied prisoners.

Fearing that the British would make landings on the Norwegian coast, Hitler moved 10,000 troops there on 5 April and marched towards

Finnish troops on manoeuvres.

April 1940: the German destroyer *Georg Thiele* after the Second Battle of Narvik.

Denmark – to the astonishment of the Danish authorities, who had believed diplomatic assurances from the Nazis that their neutrality would be respected. The Danish prime minister Torvald Stauning was so certain of this that he refused to mobilize, in case it provoked the Germans.

But Hitler needed no provocation. Early on 9 April, his stormtroopers crossed the Danish frontier. Even so, many Danish officials refused to believe this was a 'real' invasion, and the Danish naval commander-in-chief could not bring himself to order his ships to open fire. Realizing it was too late to resist, King Christian X ordered an immediate cease-fire. By 6.25 am, all fighting had stopped and Denmark was under Nazi control. Only 13 Danish soldiers had been killed and just two German planes shot down.

Norwegian officials in Oslo were also taken by surprise as German commandos arrived in the city and in Trondheim, Bergen and Narvik. The invaders cut the electricity supplies to the capital, and the Norwegian cabinet huddled in the dark, forced to read the German ultimatum by candlelight. With their telephones down, they sent out a general mobilization order to their armed forces by post and left the city. With 20 trucks carrying the Norwegian gold reserves, they transferred their seat of government northwards, facing a concerted attack from the German air force targeting the Norwegian king Haakon VII, who was hiding with them in a wood near the Swedish frontier.

ABOVE: The *Altmark* before its attack. OPPOSITE: After the First Narvik battle.

Reynaud heard about the invasion of Norway from the news agency Reuters – which shows how much Allied intelligence had failed. Neither he nor the British could believe the Germans had reached so far north so quickly, and were confused about how to deal with the invasion. British attempts to take Narvik and Trondheim proved abortive, while landings at the small fishing villages of Namsos and Andalsnes failed because they were within the range of the *Luftwaffe*, now operating from Norwegian airfields.

Even so, the Nazi invasion was not a complete success. Unexpected resistance from the Norwegian navy and from two Royal Navy actions cost the German navy three cruisers and ten destroyers – which left it with only three cruisers and four destroyers fit for action. Worse still for Hitler, King Haakon and his government managed to escape to London, adding a million tons of shipping to the Allied merchant fleet.

British politicians were in uproar over the setbacks. "In the name of God, go!" the elderly Conservative MP Leopold Amery bawled at Chamberlain in the House of Commons. The opposition Labour party refused to join a coalition government under Chamberlain, and by 10 May, Winston Churchill – the man responsible for the disastrous Norwegian landings – was Prime Minister.

THE FALL OF FRANCE
French and British Armies Overwhelmed

Hitler's first planned date for the invasion of France had been 12 November 1939 – to the horror of the German generals who made strenuous efforts to dissuade him. Bad weather repeatedly delayed the project – then a freak accident forced him to cancel it. A liaison officer to the German Airborne Forces commander-in-chief flying from Munster to Bonn was forced down by appalling weather, miles off course, inside Belgium. The papers he was carrying, which he failed to destroy before capture, were the complete plans for the invasion of France, and the Belgians handed these over to the Allies. It has been suggested that Nazi leaders were victims of a subtle plot by German intelligence to thwart the invasion; either way, the whole offensive had to be replanned.

The new plan was the brainchild of the young general Erich von Manstein, who suggested a strike through the Ardennes. Hitler admired the idea so much that he came to believe he had thought of it himself.

May 1940: Rotterdam after Nazi air attack.

1940: German soldiers look on while Rotterdam burns.

The Dutch military attaché in Berlin received a tip-off on 9 May 1940 that an invasion was imminent. "Tomorrow at dawn; hold tight", he signalled back to the Hague. But when Hitler attacked Holland, Belgium, Luxembourg and France simultaneously the following morning, the Dutch foreign minister Eelco van Kleffens was still debating with his colleagues what should be done.

German airborne forces attacked the Hague and Rotterdam, overwhelming the Dutch border defences to the east and seizing the main bridge in the centre of Rotterdam by sea-plane. Four days later, Rotterdam was still holding out, but when they were negotiating a surrender, they were bombed heavily from the air. Approximately 980 civilians were killed; two hours later, the city authorities gave way. When the French Seventh Army arrived in support five days later, it found that over 100,000 Dutch soldiers had already surrendered.

ABOVE: Refugees on the road in Belgium. BELOW: German paratroopers and infantry in Holland.

May 1940: the broken bridge over the Maas.

French tanks on manoeuvres before the invasion.

Exhausted Belgian troops on the Brussels road.

The German attack on Holland was not a complete success: a surprise thrust towards the Hague failed to capture the Dutch government, which escaped with the Dutch royal family by British destroyer to London.

Germany had at that stage only 4500 trained paratroopers, and nearly all were used in the attack on Holland. The remaining para-troopers were used in Belgium, their numbers augmented by dummies dropped to spread panic. A strike-force of 85 parachute-engineers landed on the roof of the heavily defended Fort Eben Emael, which guarded Liège and the Albert Canal, and captured it with the loss of only five men. Others captured key bridges to allow the German divisions to drive deep into Belgian territory.

"I have nothing to offer but blood, toil, tears and sweat," Churchill

ABOVE: French troops mobilizing in Paris. BELOW: Confusion at the Gare de l'Est in Paris, May 1940.

June 1940: German troops near the Somme.

told a sombre British House of Commons three days later.

While the attention of the Allies was diverted by the paratroop raids, the brilliant German panzer commander Heinz Guderian was heading through Luxembourg towards the Ardennes – heavily wooded terrain which had been dismissed as impassable by British, French and other German military experts alike. He took with him the greatest concentration of tanks ever seen in war; four days after the start of the offensive, he crossed the French frontier and arrived at the Meuse.

The Allied mobile divisions were deep inside Belgium and increasingly exposed by this flanking manoeuvre; there were only a few poorly equipped French tank divisions to oppose Guderian. Even so, Guderian realized he must cross the Meuse quickly before the French regrouped. Protected by 12 squadrons of dive-bombers, he made the crossing near Sedan and, brushing aside the fears of his own commanders (even Hitler had been expecting a French counter-attack on Guderian's now-exposed flank), pressed north. Opposition crumbled before him. "We have lost the battle," Reynaud told Churchill on the phone on 15 May.

Churchill flew to Paris the following day, to find the roads south blocked by refugees, and the army command in confusion. In a desperate attempt to inspire them, he promised 10 fighter squadrons – a promise blocked by his own cabinet back home after warnings that air defences for Britain were wearing dangerously thin. "Where is the strategic reserve?" Churchill asked the Supreme Commander Gamelin. "There is none," came the reply.

The young brigadier Charles de Gaulle was sent to test out his theories of tank warfare using a hastily assembled counter-attacking force on 17 May. He was harried by dive-bombers and his 150 tanks were pushed back to Laon, but after his brave stand he was asked to join Reynaud's government as under-secretary for war. "I felt myself borne up by a limitless fury," he wrote. "It's too stupid. If I live I will fight wherever I must, as long as I must, until the enemy is defeated and the national stain is washed clear."

By 20 May, Guderian had reached the sea at Abbeville, and was turning towards the Channel ports and the British army which faced the German divisions advancing on its other flank. At Gravelines, just ten miles from Dunkirk – the last point of escape for the British troops – Guderian's panzers were halted by orders from German high command.

Meanwhile, Reynaud had sacked Gamelin, and was forced to wait three days for his successor Maxime Weygand to arrive from Syria. When Weygand arrived, he immediately proposed an Allied counter-attack. Gort accordingly made a strike south from Arras with two tank battalions. This was highly successful at first, but by the time the French arrived in support, only two tanks were left in working order, and the British were

Guderian pushes through France.

The remains of a German Heinkel III in France.

ABOVE: A French motorcycle unit. OPPOSITE: Panzers at the Meuse in France.

Panzers rumble through devastated towns in Northern France.

German troops clear road-blocks in the Ardennes.

A German panzer crew-member stops for a break during the headlong advance.

A panzer on the outskirts of Paris.

An abandoned French armoured car.

forced to pull back. Even so, German high command had received a scare, and the army was ordered to suspend its advance and consolidate its gains.

Or was the German halt, as some historians have suggested, a ploy by Hitler to facilitate a peace agreement with Britain? We will never know for sure, but whatever the reason, the destruction of British and French forces at Dunkirk was left in the hands of Goering's *Luftwaffe*. It failed to complete the job.

The three day pause in the German advance was all the British needed to escape. On the evening of 25 May, Gort decided to defy the instructions issued by his new Supreme Commander Weygand to hold fast. With the reluctant agreement of the British cabinet, he began the evacuation from the beaches of Dunkirk.

The Belgians, meanwhile, had been fighting desperately in a situation confused by refugees and sketch-maps of their parlous situation dropped by German planes. "The great battle which we feared has begun," said the Belgian king Leopold to his troops. But in spite of desperate pleas from the British to hang on until their forces made their escape, Leopold announced a surrender on 28 May.

The Belgian government, now in Paris, refused to accept the king's decision – but their reserves had lasted just long enough to save

King Leopold of Belgium.

June 1940: German troops march through the Arc de Triomphe.

Goosestepping through the heart of Paris.

Gort. Although Churchill was preparing people for the worst, the Royal Navy – aided by 860 pleasure boats, fishing smacks, canal barges and dingys – ferried 200,000 British and 140,000 French soldiers to England. The evacuation was hailed as a victory of sorts by the British, but seen as a betrayal by the French command, who believed they had been deserted at a crucial moment of the campaign. The British lost six destroyers and 177 fighter planes in the operation; the troops had left most of their weapons and equipment behind on the beaches. As many as 150,000 French troops in the rearguard were captured.

Shortly afterwards, Weygand's attempt to hold the line at the Somme was swept aside in a new German offensive, while the French government escaped to Tours, then Bordeaux. On 14 June, the first German troops marched along the Champs-Elysées in Paris. As they did so, a declaration by Mussolini brought Italy into the war, and he ordered his troops to attack France from the south in the hope of a place at the negotiating table.

Churchill, Halifax and the press magnate Lord Beaverbrook – now the minister of aircraft production – met the French government for the last time in Tours in 13 June, with Reynaud's mistress in the background urging a French surrender. An offer of union between France and Britain, made by Churchill, was rejected by the French cabinet. Reynaud's suggestion that the cabinet form a government in exile in America was also rejected, and he resigned. His replacement was the 84-year-old hero of Verdun, Marshal Philippe Pétain.

On 21 June, Pétain asked the Germans for an armistice. When he

Dictating terms in the railway coach at Compiègne.

June 1940: the bombardment of Dunkirk.

Abandoned British AA guns at Dunkirk.

British troops on the beach under air attack.

heard of the request, Hitler's face, according to the American reporter William Shirer, was "afire with scorn, anger, hate, revenge, triumph". He insisted that the agreement be signed in the same railway carriage at Compiègne where German generals had signed surrender terms in 1918. It was agreed that a French government, based in Vichy, would be allowed to administer the country south of the Loire.

A few days later, the Vichy government was made to pay for its accomodation with the Nazis. Fearing that Pétain had made a secret deal with the Nazis and concerned at the prospect of the French fleet falling into German hands, Churchill ordered the destruction of French battleships at Oran, Algeria. It was, he said, the "most hateful decision" he had ever had to make. Pétain immediately broke off diplomatic relations with

Britain and ordered a symbolic bombing of the island of Gibraltar.

Vichy wallowed in self-recrimination over the French defeat. "It's the fault of socialist school-teachers," said Pétain, who allowed Pierre Laval and Raphael Alibert to put Reynaud and Daladier under arrest and install an authoritarian and virulently anti-semitic régime. For the next four years, the Vichy government veered between tacit endorsement of Nazi policies and active collaboration.

The Battle of France, as it came to be known, had enormous consequences for all participants. The French army had been all but destroyed and France itself divided; and such was the speed of his victory that Hitler became convinced his armies were invincible – an over-confidence that would later prove disastrous in Russia and North Africa. Last and by no means least, over 10 million civilians had been dispos-

Dunkirk: soldiers wade out to a troopship.

sessed. It was their fate to trudge miserably along the roads of western Europe, their belongings heaped on carts, sometimes collapsing with exhaustion, often strafed by the *Luftwaffe*.

And across the English Channel, though elated by the miracle of Dunkirk, it was slowly dawning on the British that nothing stood between Hitler and European domination but 23 miles of seawater.

After the evacuation: trucks abandoned on the Dunkirk beaches.

THE ISLAND FORTRESS

The Battle of Britain and the Blitz

"We shall defend our island, whatever the cost may be," vowed Churchill in his elation and relief at the escape at Dunkirk. But though the British were by this time able to break some of the German Enigma codes, and knew that no immediate invasion was planned, their ability to withstand one in the future looked slight. During the Battle of France, almost as many British planes had been lost as had rolled off the production lines; while much of the army's artillery and armour had been left behind on the beaches at Dunkirk.

Desperate measures had to be taken. A general conscription was ordered and, by the beginning of October, 1.7 million Britons had joined the armed forces. A Home Guard was formed, although because of the weapons shortage they had to be armed with props from theatre companies and even with Napoleonic pikes taken from Admiral Nelson's 150-year-old wooden flagship, *Victory*, in Portsmouth Harbour.

ABOVE: **Messerschmitt Bf 109 fighters returning from a raid on Kent.** RIGHT: **A Spitfire banking.**

German commanders watch troops training for Operation Sea Lion, the planned invasion of Britain.

At the same time, high-ranking officials put out feelers via Swedish diplomats to see if some kind of agreement could be reached to end the war. It is thought that the former prime minister David Lloyd George and former king Edward VIII, now Duke of Windsor, might have been pre-pared to lead a defeated Britain. It is also possible that certain British aristocrats considered handing over Malta and other British colonies to placate Hitler. But Churchill was adamant that Britain should stand firm, and refused to consider the idea.

In a speech made in the Reichstag on 19 July, Hitler warned Britain of "unending suffering and misery" if they rejected his peace terms. Churchill gave Halifax, one of the architects of appeasement, the job of spurning the offer on radio. A few days later, Operation Sea Lion, the proposed invasion of Britain, was fixed for 15 September.

German chiefs-of-staff were worried about the invasion plans. The German navy was inadequate to the task, and they suspected that cross-ing the Channel might only be possible after the *Luftwaffe* had gained air supremacy over Britain. Goering promised to bring this about in a mat-ter of weeks and, on 13 August, the so-called Battle of Britain began.

The first day was to set the pattern for the succeeding months. Wave upon wave of the *Luftwaffe*'s bombers, escorted by fighters, overflew

British airfields, ports and other tactical targets, sustaining losses in a ratio of roughly two to one.

Although they were heavily outnumbered, the British had several clear advantages. They were operating over home territory, so the Spitfires and Hurricanes could attack, land and refuel, and fly up to attack again. They had radar, which allowed them to track the approach of the German bombers. They had a new minister for aircraft production, the press baron Lord Beaverbrook, appointed by Churchill in May, who managed to out-perform the German factories. And they also had a simple, clear objective – the destruction of as many German bombers as possible – while Goering changed his objectives on numerous occasions, denting the morale of German pilots.

The morale of the RAF, on the other hand, strengthened as the battle progressed. "Never in the field of human conflict," said Churchill in his tribute to the airmen, "has so much been owed by so many to so few". Even so, the British suffered from a serious shortage of trained pilots.

August 1940: the British Home Guard – then the Local Defence Volunteers – in training.

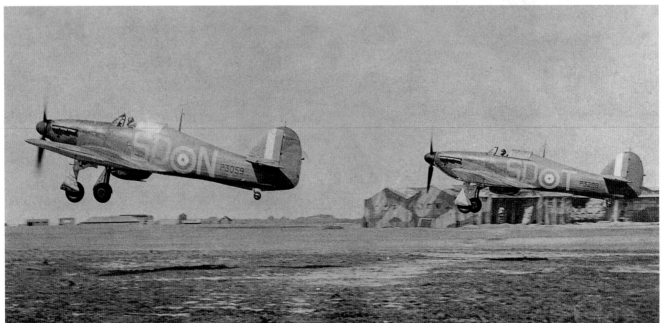

TOP: Spitfires in attack formation. ABOVE: Hurricanes 'scramble' to intercept raiders.

RAF fighter pilots 'scramble'.

A quiet moment at the front-line RAF airfield of Biggin Hill.

Bullet holes in a downed Junkers 88 near the English coast.

Dorniers over the London docks.

Those that survived found themselves under increasing strain, and fighting alongside new recruits with less and less experience. And they had no means of countering the effective German attacks on their fighter airfields in Kent.

Then, by one of the strange twists of war, these attacks were suddenly called off. A German bomber, lost on its way home on 24 August, accidentally bombed London, and Churchill responded with a series of small raids on Berlin. Hitler was outraged, having promised that no such thing was possible, and switched his attack to the indiscriminate bombing of British cities – a strategy which both sides then adopted for the rest of the war. The British airfields were saved: by the end of the battle in October, the Germans had lost 1733 aircraft to the British 915.

In the same month, Hitler postponed the invasion of Britain for the winter. The mass bombing of British cities, the so-called 'Blitz', destroyed three and a half million homes and killed 30,000 people. Coventry was all but demolished on 14 November; a massive raid on the night of 29 December destroyed eight of London's historic Wren churches and forced firefighters to blow up buildings to create fire-breaks – something not done since the Great Fire of 1666. Soon British civilian bomb disposal groups were having to defuse up to 4000 unexploded bombs a month. "I feel we are fighting for life, and survive from day to day and hour to hour," said Churchill in Parliament.

But these terror tactics, far from destroying the moral fibre of the British population, only seemed to reinforce their will to endure. It was a lesson apparently lost on British Bomber Command, which was itself to pursue a policy of terror-bombing on Germany until the final weeks of the war.

By June 1941, the German air attacks on Britain had become more half-hearted as Goering switched his attention to preparing for war in the East. Meanwhile, a bitter personal battle in the British Air Ministry between Hugh Dowding and Keith Park – the two men responsible for winning the Battle of Britain – resulted in their removal from command.

Britain's island status allowed it to hold out against the German invasion, but only because the sea-lanes to America were kept open – just –

ABOVE: Southwark in flames during the Blitz. BELOW: The remains of Balham underground station.

LEFT: January 1941 – ruined London seen from St Paul's. **ABOVE:** Fire-hoses snake down a street following a raid.

ABOVE: Firemen working in the rubble of London's East End.

ABOVE: A British family carrying gas masks go into their new air raid shelter. BELOW: Children await evacuation.

for vital food and supplies. Hitler realized this, and as far back as September 1939, his U-boats had been ordered to sink as much tonnage as possible to starve Britain into submission.

The so-called Battle of the Atlantic had begun with the sinking of the British liner *Athenia* on 4 September 1939, and the dropping of magnetic mines around the coast of Britain. But after the fall of Western Europe, the naval war assumed a new intensity. The French Atlantic ports suddenly became available to the Germans, and Italy's 118 submarines roved the Mediterranean. At the same time, badly needed ships were taken off Atlantic escort duty – despite protests from the British admiral Sir Charles Forbes – and sent to southern England to wait for the expected invasion.

In July 1940 alone, nearly 500,000 tons of shipping was sunk in the Atlantic. The German code-breakers had taught themselves to read British naval signals, so they knew many of the convoy sailings, routes and plans. The U-boat commander Karl Doenitz was able to direct his submarines with unerring accuracy. He worked out that

Londoners take shelter in the Underground.

the British would be forced to surrender if he could sink 750,000 tons of shipping a month. The British shared his view: they put the figure at 600,000 tons.

But submarines were slow and the distances were enormous: many convoys were able to slip past. Hitler had also given less priority to building U-boats than Admiral Doenitz would have liked, and by the end of 1940 only 22 were operational. On the other hand, U-boat commanders had developed lethal new tactics, operating together in 'wolf packs'; and the exploits of submarine aces such as Otto Kretschmer and Gunther Prien (who had sunk the *Royal Oak*) proved inspirational to many other U-boat commanders.

U-boat ace Otto Kretschmer.

The British were forced to find methods of fighting back. Using still-rudimentary sonar detection equipment, destroyers and corvettes dropped depth-charges on suspected U-boats, and by March 1941, Prien had been sunk and Kretschmer captured. Both ended their careers in running battles with the same convoy, and before he sank, Kretschmer – determined to be the first U-Boat commander to sink 300,000 tons of shipping – ordered his radio operator to signal Doenitz that he had sunk another 50,000 tons. The man who had sunk the *Athenia,* Julius Lemp, was also captured by the British, together with crucial code material which allowed them to crack the German naval codes.

Help also arrived in the form of the lend-lease legislation passed in America. US president Franklin Roosevelt promised the British 50 elderly American destroyers in return for strategic British bases and other trade concessions. When the ships were delivered in September 1940, only nine were fit for immediate service, but it was an important symbolic gesture from Roosevelt, who was battling the powerful isolationist lobby who wanted to keep America out of the war.

Safely elected for his third term of office at the end of 1940, Roosevelt could be even more helpful to the British. American troops marched into Iceland to relieve the British forces there, and soon American destroyers were themselves being attacked by U-boats.

"In March and April, a naval warfare will start such as the enemy has never expected," vowed Hitler in 1941. "Wherever British ships cruise, our U-boats will be sent against them until the hour for decision arrives." As it was, April 1941 saw nearly 700,000 tons of shipping go to the bottom of the Atlantic. It was probably the moment when Britain came closest to losing the war.

There was also the threat of German surface raiders – pocket battleships, battlecruisers and converted merchant ships – though the main fleet was carefully conserved by Hitler, afraid of the propaganda reverse any major losses would bring. In January 1941, the German battlecruisers *Scharnhorst* and *Gneisenau* slipped into the Atlantic via the Denmark Strait, and after a successful cruise attacking convoys and avoiding

Gunther Prien on the conning tower.

battle themselves, slipped into the French port of Brest.

Encouraged by this success, in May 1941 the German naval commander Erich Raeder ordered a repeat exercise using the powerful new pocket battleship, *Bismarck*. Under the command of Gunther Lutjens, who had masterminded the *Scharnhorst* and *Gneisenau* raids, the *Bismarck* slipped from its anchorage in a Norwegian fjord and headed for the convoy routes.

German Grand Admiral Raeder.

Alerted by the threat to merchant shipping, the British Home Fleet went after the raider. In a short engagement, the British battlecruiser *Hood* took a direct hit in its armoury and exploded; only three of its crew survived. But on 28 May, as it headed for Brest, the *Bismarck* was finally trapped and sunk. Hundreds of German sailors were drowned when a U-boat scare forced rescuing British ships away from the scene. "The *Bismarck* put up a gallant fight

Arctic conditions on a British convoy.

Royal Navy destroyers on convoy duty.

Helping the Russian war effort – an impromptu rally at an English port.

May 1941: the *Bismarck* returns the fire of the British Fleet.

against impossible odds," wrote the British admiral, Sir John Tovey, in his report. "It is unfortunate that 'for political reasons' this fact cannot be made public."

Hitler was said to be "melancholy beyond words" over the sinking; and he had another reason for concern. The day before the *Bismarck* went down, the first fully escorted British convoy left Newfoundland: it seemed that the 'happy time' for U-boat commanders was about to end.

Neither by air nor sea were the Nazis able to bring Britain to its knees. If an invasion of the island had been successful, there is every reason to think the Nazis would have installed the kind of régime that had become the norm in occupied Europe. Liberal intellectuals would have been arrested (a list of 2820 had already been drawn up), Jews would have been 'transported' and slavery instituted; there would have been both collaboration and resistance.

The British were fortunate not to have to undergo the long night of occupation, in which neighbour mistrusted neighbour and survival was often merely a matter of chance.

LIFE IN THE REICH

Tyranny and Persecution in Occupied Europe

Shortly after Marshal Pétain signed the armistice with Hitler's generals, 49 year-old General Charles de Gaulle flew to London from Bordeaux, passing over a sinking British troopship in the Bay of Biscay. At 6 pm, 18 June 1940, the future leader of the Free French Army made his famous radio speech to the French people – a call to arms received with dismay by the new Vichy government. "Whatever happens, the flame of French resistance must not and cannot die," he said. Meanwhile in Paris, a triumphant Hitler was visiting the tomb of Napoleon. "I am grateful to fate," he said solemnly.

Although acts of genocide had already taken place in occupied Poland, the conquered peoples of western Europe were still unsure what to expect of their new overlords. They were not left in the dark for long. The Nazi commissar of Holland, Arthur Seyss-Inquart, promised to main-

Strange bedfellows – Marshal Pétain with Hermann Goering.

A Gestapo guard watches over Polish 'suspects'.

De Gaulle on a British warship.

tain Dutch laws where possible, but warned ominously: "Of course we do not consider Jews to be Dutch".

Under Nazi occupation, French citizens had no right to listen to the BBC, read 'non-Aryan' or 'subversive' literature, send cables or travel freely; they had to abide by a 7 pm curfew. In Holland, on the other hand, the word 'royal' was excised from street names and prayers and priests were specifically forbidden to preach on the text of Psalm 130 – "Out of the depths have I cried unto thee, Oh Lord." Further north, to add insult to injury, the people of Norway were told they would have to pay the costs of the Nazi occupation.

There were acts of passive resistance. Norwegian history teachers went on unanimous strike and Danish students sported the colours of the RAF; the Danish king even sent telegrams of sympathy to police who had been wounded in a riot involving 300 local Nazis. But these shows of outrage, while courageous, had small effect – and could sometimes

The citizens of Prague settle down to Nazi rule.

backfire. When the members of the Norwegian supreme court resigned in protest at Nazi administered justice, they were simply replaced by more malleable functionaries.

At the same time, the collaborators began to step forward. One of the most infamous was the Norwegian, Vidkun Quisling. As the Nazis invaded his country in 1940, Quisling tricked his way into a radio studio and announced that he had assumed control. Though Hitler got rid of him six days later, he was reinstated as puppet leader in 1942.

The governments of conquered countries, no matter how distasteful they found the Nazis, were in an intolerable position: every official measure had to be taken with Nazi consent. It is unlikely that Marshal Pétain himself realized the full implications of, as he phrased it, the "path of collaboration". The Vichy government was soon forced to pay for the German occupation of northern France, while Pétain's chosen deputy, Pierre Laval, began to consort openly with fascists in an attempt to sideline the old warrior.

'Culture war': German soldiers sightseeing in Prague.

For ordinary men and women, too, the price of occupation soon became clear. By the end of 1940, the first telegrams arrived in Warsaw announcing the deaths of family members in concentration camps. Partisans and ethnic 'undesirables' were summarily shot. Non-germanic people were forced *en masse* from their homes to make way for incoming 'Aryan' families. When a German soldier was shot and killed in the Paris metro on 20 April 1941 (Hitler's 52nd birthday), 22 civilian hostages were executed as a reprisal, their fate blazoned on posters throughout the city.

In London, a number of organisations were formed to subvert Nazi rule. The Special Operations Executive (SOE) was the most prominent of these; its mission, Churchill told his minister for economic warfare

ABOVE: Partisans pay the terrible price of resistance. OPPOSITE: Night-life in occupied Paris.

Hugh Dalton, was to "set Europe ablaze". The SOE began sending trained agents to Europe to forge links with emerging resistance groups.

Radio broadcasting was also given high priority. The BBC and the British Foreign Office co-operated in the creation of the European Service, a mouthpiece for the exiles of the occupied countries and an inspirational news source. Its director, Noel Newsome, was in charge of broadcasts across three networks in more than 20 languages. Newsome was convinced that wartime news was most effective as propaganda when it contained a 'moral core'. "Would you risk your life to listen to that?" he scrawled on official scripts, demanding that those Europeans who listened in secrecy to illegal wirelesses deserved the truth. "It is not enough to show ourselves smart by exposing [lies] and the Nazis stupid by perpetrating them so clumsily," Newsome wrote. "We must go much further and show that these frauds are the inevitable manifestations of a fraudulent system, of a system which is a fake to

Noel Newsome at the BBC.

"La Gazette Officielle"

REWARD OF £25

A REWARD OF £25 WILL BE GIVEN TO THE PERSON WHO FIRST GIVES TO THE INSPECTOR OF POLICE INFORMATION LEADING TO THE CONVICTION OF ANYONE (NOT ALREADY DISCOVERED) FOR THE OFFENCE OF MARKING ON ANY GATE, WALL OR OTHER PLACE WHATSOEVER VISIBLE TO THE PUBLIC THE LETTER "V" OR ANY OTHER SIGN OR ANY WORD OR WORDS CALCULATED TO OFFEND THE GERMAN AUTHORITIES OR SOLDIERS.

THIS 8th DAY OF JULY, 1941.

VICTOR G. CAREY,

Bailiff.

ABOVE: Local officials in occupied Guernsey were forced to toe the line. BELOW: German troops at Notre Dame de Paris.

A German checkpoint in provincial France.

its very core, a sham which by its very nature cannot endure."

For their part, the Nazi propagandists were hamstrung both by their fear of departing from the 'official line' and by outright political interference. Hitler himself ruled at one point that the name 'Winston Churchill' should never be used without the epithet 'whisky-drinking'.

Newsome also initiated the 'V for Victory' campaign, first used by the BBC Belgian service at the beginning of 1941. Within weeks it was clear that the campaign had been an enormous success: all over occupied Europe, 'V' symbols were being chalked on walls while taxi drivers honked out the signature tune of the campaign.

Its impact was such that Goebbels made an unsuccessful attempt to co-opt it, claiming V stood for the old German word *Viktoria*; he also ordered a large 'V' symbol to be hung from the Eiffel Tower. The European Service responded in kind: the truth, they said, was that the German 'V' stood for *Vergeltung* – persecution.

MUSSOLINI'S MISADVENTURES

Italian Defeats in Greece and Africa

Mussolini's main motivation in declaring war on Britain and France was his fear of missing out on a chair at the peace conference. "It is the struggle of fruitful young people against sterile people on the threshold of their decline," he declared on 10 June 1940. Intoxicated by his bombast, blackshirted Italian youths swarmed into the streets shouting: "Nice, Corsica, Tunis, Suez!"

Jealous of the gains made by his fascist ally in northern Europe, Mussolini unwisely manufactured a war with Greece. On 28 October, Italian troops in summer uniforms crossed the frontier into a wintry battleground – and immediately ran into difficulties with the Greek army, which pushed his inexperienced soldiers back into Albania. Even so, Mussolini's entry into the war was a threat to British possessions in

Mussolini accepts the surrender of a Bedouin tribesman in Libya.

Columns of Italian PoW's march to a lengthy stay behind barbed wire.

New Zealand soldiers with a captured Italian flag.

German Ju-52 transports arriving at Italian airfields.

Italian troops crawling under British barbed wire defences.

Empire and Greek troops deployed there, 50,000 had to be evacuated in the face of the German advance. Among the evacuees were the Greek government and the king.

Much of the Middle East was now threatened. Iraqi troops attacked the British air bases around Baghdad, and the Vichy government allowed the Germans to use their air bases in Syria. The one bright moment for the Allies occurred at the Battle of Cape Matapan on 27 March. Helped by readings of Italian naval codes, the British Mediterranean Fleet ambushed and utterly destroyed an Italian naval force.

The British troops evacuated from Greece now massed in Crete,

November 1941: disconsolate Italian prisoners outside Tobruk.

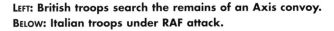

LEFT: British troops search the remains of an Axis convoy.
BELOW: Italian troops under RAF attack.

'defended' from air bases 300 miles away in Egypt. Believing their forces to be relatively safe now because the Royal Navy controlled the sea, their leaders did not anticipate a threat from the air. "Cannot understand nervousness; am not in the least anxious about airborne attack," signalled the Allied commander, New Zealand general Sir Bernard Freyberg, before the first reports of German paratroopers came through on the 20 May. In fact, 3000 had landed on the island, taking strongpoints and spearheading major beach landings. "Victory in Crete essential at this turning point of the war," signalled Churchill – but it was too late. Confused and demoralized, the British withdrew to the island's

BELOW: March 1941 – the Italian fleet before Matapan.

ABOVE: May 1941 – Paratroop General Kurt Student in Crete.
OPPOSITE: German panzers below the Acropolis, Athens.

German parachutes fill the skies over Crete.

German mountain troops disembark in Crete.

The British cruiser *York* beached in Crete.

southern beaches, where they were evacuated to Egypt by the Royal Navy. But three cruisers and six destroyers were sunk by German dive-bombers during the evacuation: in the panic as many as 13,000 British troops had to be left behind.

Successful though the Crete operation had been, the Germans also sustained heavy losses. Hitler therefore rejected plans put forward by the airborne commander, General Kurt Student, to use the same paratroop tactics to capture Cyprus and the Suez Canal.

The Führer might have been wise at this point to exploit Allied confusion in the Middle East. De Gaulle had been wrong in believing that Vichy forces there would answer his call to turn on the Axis forces, and British and French troops found themselves fighting each other in Syria. On the other hand, a group of Free French foreign legionnaires, besieged by the Italians in Bir Hakeim in the Libyan desert, broke out and, after fierce fighting, reached the British lines. They included the future French prime minister, Pierre Messmer.

In East Africa there was no such confusion: British forces were steadily driving out the Italians, and the Italian commander, the Duke of Aosta, surrendered there on 19 May. Two weeks before that, the Emperor of Abyssinia, Haile Selassie, was flown back to his capital Addis Ababa accompanied by the unconventional British guerilla leader, Orde Wingate.

But in Libya, Wavell's counter-attack on Rommel, known as Operation Battle-Axe, was halted by the Germans' destructive use of 88mm anti-aircraft guns against the lightly armoured British tanks. On 21 June 1941, Churchill ordered General Sir Claude Auchinleck to make way for General Wavell as Allied commander in the Middle East.

General Auchinleck talks to the press.

BARBAROSSA

Hitler's Armies Invade Stalin's Russia

The Nazi invasion of Soviet Russia was probably the single most momentous event of World War II. Despite the cynicism of the Molotov-Ribbentrop pact, Hitler had always distrusted Stalin, and the Communists had always been seen as the Nazis' true ideological enemies. Hitler needed land in the East for his longed-for *Lebensraum*. And there were strategic reasons for an invasion. In June 1940, Stalin's troops had marched into Romania to take back the former Russian province of Bessarabia: they were dangerously close to the Romanian oilfields on which Hitler's war in the West depended. Romanian support for Hitler's invasion of Soviet Russia was linked to an agreement to return the province to them.

Nonetheless, Hitler had first to overcome the unease of many of his generals: Napoleon's catastrophic adventure on Russian soil was, after all, a staple lesson of every military school. But Hitler managed to convince them that an invasion was simply a pre-emptive strike, and that

The sufferings caused by Operation Barbarossa.

August 1941: German columns near Minsk.

sooner or later Stalin would order his 'barbarian hordes' to march westwards. If German forces managed to destroy the Red Army quickly enough, he insisted, and the principal cities could be taken, the Russians would be unable to regroup and would be forced to come to terms. The generals were also persuaded of the superiority of their armed forces: they had seen for themselves the damage that the lightly equipped Finns had managed to inflict on the Russians.

For his part, Stalin was totally unprepared. Many of his best generals had already been murdered in various pre-war purges; and he ignored detailed information given him by the Soviet spy Richard Sorge, working from Tokyo where officials were being kept in touch with German preparations. The Soviet leader assumed that Hitler would not attack until he had successfully invaded Britain; the British in turn passed on a correct prediction for the date of an attack on Russia.

Operation Barbarossa began on 22 June 1941 – the day before the anniversary of Napoleon's invasion of 1812. Over 3,000,000 men, 7100 guns and 3300 tanks were deployed across a 930-mile front. There was no declaration of war.

General Wilhelm Ritter von Leeb led the Northern Army Group into Lithuania, Fedor von Bock's Central Army Group struck through Poland towards Moscow, and General Gerd von Rundstedt took the Southern Army Group towards the Ukraine. The Red Army was to be trapped in the heartland of Russia by a gigantic pincer movement. "I have decided again today to place the fate and future of the Reich and our people in

Stormtroopers hitch a ride on a self-propelled gun.

A Russian village in flames.

almost as peculiar as the previous alliance between Stalin and Hitler. "If Hitler invaded hell," said Churchill, "I should at least make a favourable reference to the Devil in the House of Commons."

Stalin appealed for help from the beginning, and although the British refused to open a second front in Europe at this stage, Lord Beaverbrook ran the gauntlet of opposition from the services and agreed to divert some American resources to Russia instead. On 28 September, the first Arctic convoy left Iceland bound for Archangel: British and American convoys would shortly be providing large amounts of equipment to the Soviets – including 600,000 pairs of army boots a month. Churchill's wife Clementine launched the Aid for Russia appeal.

Support for Russia was intensified by stories of Nazi atrocities in occupied territory, and by Churchill's assertion that "since the Mongol invasions of Europe in the 16th century, there has never been methodical, merciless butchery on such a scale."

This was no exaggeration. Massacres of Jews followed in every town

A German anti-tank gun in action.

that was captured, sometimes with the enthusiastic involvement of local fascists. In just three days in August, over 23,000 were murdered in Kamenets Podolsk in the Ukraine; while in Odessa on 22 October, as many as 25,000 were herded into four enormous warehouses and burned to death.

The appalling treatment of civilians by German forces also alienated possible allies – those disaffected Belorussians and Ukrainians who had at first welcomed them with flowers, kisses and vodka.

By the end of September 1941, the Germans were ready to carry on

Hard-driven German troops pause for rations.

their advance towards Moscow: German journalists were told to prepare announcements of its fall. "The enemy is broken and will never be in a position to rise again," announced Hitler in a public address. Not for the first time, he spoke too soon.

It was true that as many as eight Russian armies were destroyed as they defended the capital, and that Moscow civilians panicked as they tried to leave the city; but though the government was moved to Kuibyshev, Stalin remained to take the salute for a military parade to celebrate the 1917 revolution. Meanwhile, 500,000 Russian civilians dug 5000 miles of defensive ditches around the city. The German attack stalled.

Worse for Hitler, winter was setting in. By November, the temperature around Moscow had dropped to -31 degrees Fahrenheit. Even oil froze, and German tank crews had to light

A German anti-tank gun and propelled gun mount a road-block.

fires under their vehicles for up to four hours before they could be put into action. At the same time they had to deal with the new Soviet tank, the heavily armed and highly mobile T-34.

General Zhukov had also been reinforced by 25 divisions from the Far East; in the south, Russian troops recaptured Rostov. The sensible precaution for Hitler would have been to delay his advance on Moscow until warmer weather, but since victory had already been announced, he feared a major propanganda reverse. The Germans pressed on, reaching the Moscow tram terminus on 2 December. The Kremlin was visible in the distance.

But three days later, Zhukov ordered his own troops into the offensive. Determined not to risk any kind of retreat through the icy wastes, Hitler ordered his troops to stand firm. For many of them, the consequences were disastrous: they froze to death or were overrun when their weaponry became congealed with ice.

Before Christmas, a furious Hitler sacked all his group commanders in the operation and named himself as army commander-in-chief.

THE BIG THREE

AMERICA, BRITAIN AND RUSSIA JOIN FORCES

THE SLEEPING GIANT

America's Isolation Brought to an End

The US envoy to Britain, Harry Hopkins, was impressed by British morale during the Blitz. "If courage alone can win, the results are inevitable," he reported to President Roosevelt. But he added, "They need our help desperately."

Hopkins had been sent to Britain in January 1941 because of the increasingly depressing reports of the American ambassador – John. F. Kennedy's father, Joseph – about the possibility of British defeat. Hopkins arrived just as Roosevelt's Lend-Lease legislation, which granted the president powers to provide equipment to assist any country he thought vital to the 'defence' of the USA, was passed. However, many Americans, most prominently Kennedy and the air hero Charles Lindbergh, opposed Lend-Lease. They believed Roosevelt wanted to lure the USA into war – and when, in June 1941, he froze all German and Italian assets, their suspicions seemed confirmed. The president had anyway been at the end of a 'charm offensive' from Churchill, who sent him regular confidential messages, bombarded him with news updates, and urged him to take a more active role on behalf of the beleaguered Allies.

Meanwhile, a secret group of British and American officials were discussing what to do if Churchill's encouragements succeeded. Secrecy was vital not only because of the potential Axis reaction, but because the US public were themselves deeply suspicious of any attempts to draw them into a European war. "Whoa, Mr President!" began one newspaper leader column, having detected a more bellicose tone to one of Roosevelt's speeches.

But events in the Atlantic were to prove beyond the control of press and politicians alike. On 10 April 1941, the US destroyer *Nitblack* attacked a U-boat which had just sunk a Dutch freighter; six months later, another destroyer, *Reuben James*, was torpedoed and sunk with the loss of all its crew. "Hitler's torpedo was directed at every American," said Roosevelt – but still he held back from war. For Hitler's invasion of Soviet Russia had been a setback for 'interventionists' like himself: Americans were prepared to send aid to a democratic country such as Britain, but it

Roosevelt reviews the US fleet in San Francisco Bay.

130

Roosevelt and Churchill in Quebec with the Earl of Athlone.

would take a miracle to make them suppliers to, or allies of, Communists.

For the moment, then, the British had to make do with American naval support alone – an understanding reached in August 1941, when Churchill and Roosevelt met on board the Royal Navy battleship *Prince of Wales* in Placentia Bay, Newfoundland. But little headway was made by the British prime minister in his efforts to secure a number of other guarantees of protection.

Yet where Churchill's 'charm offensive' failed in its objectives, the Japanese succeeded with an all-out assault. On 7 December 1941, their aircraft attacked Pearl Harbor – and America was at war in the Pacific. The next day, Churchill declared war on the Japanese, ahead of the American declaration by Congress. The other British allies followed, including China which formally declared war against both Japan and Germany.

On 11 December, there was even better news as far as Britain was concerned: Hitler declared war on the USA. He might have delayed, hoping that America expended its fury on Japan alone; but it seems likely he was convinced the USA was about to enter the war against him anyway. For his part, Churchill knew that US involvement in Europe would mean eventual victory. "That night," he wrote, "being saturated and satiated with emotion and sensation, I went to bed and slept the sleep of the saved and thankful."

But the USA was comparatively unprepared for war. Fighting the Japanese was one matter. As for Europe – should US forces attack in Africa, Italy or France first? And could strategic bombing alone win the war, as the British and American air force commanders believed?

These issues had to be resolved quickly; to do so Churchill went to Washington to urge Roosevelt to boost industrial production and help set out some kind of general strategy. New Year's Day, 1942, saw the publication of a joint declaration by the two leaders in Washington, endorsed by 26 countries calling themselves the United Nations, to "ensure life, liberty, independence and religious freedom, and to preserve the rights of man and justice".

Churchill needed the US to act decisively, for the early months of 1942

Roosevelt with his Secretary of State, Cordell Hull.

ABOVE AND LEFT: June 1942 – air raids on the vital British stronghold of Malta.

Anti-aircraft gunners in action in Malta.

August 1942: the aftermath of the Dieppe raid.

British and Canadian prisoners in Dieppe.

Exhausted commandos return to Newhaven after the Dieppe disaster.

were hard for Britain. Not only did it have dwindling food and coal reserves, but Singapore had been lost to the Japanese and the island of Malta, bomb-battered and starving, was seriously threatened in the Mediterranean. The prime minister's leadership was coming in for increasing public criticism.

The first Arctic convoys were now taking supplies to the Russians at Archangel. To threaten them, Hitler ordered *Scharnhorst* and *Gneisenau* to make a dash through the English Channel to Norway, where the *Bismarck*'s sister ship, *Tirpitz*, joined them. Afraid that these surface raiders had put to sea, the British naval chief Sir Dudley Pound ordered convoy PQ 17 to scatter. As many as 24 out of the convoy's 35 merchant

ABOVE: A U-boat commander with the Knight's Cross. LEFT: *Tirpitz* in Kaafjord.

ships were picked off by U-boats – and all, as it turned out, because of a false alarm.

The British needed to strike back to boost public morale. In March 1942, commandos successfully attacked the only Atlantic dry dock capable of taking *Tirpitz* – St Nazaire on the French coast. Five months later, a bigger force of commandos and infantry from Britain, Canada and the USA attacked the port of Dieppe. It was a catastrophe; 1000 men were killed and 2000 taken prisoner. But it provided Allied planners with vital information about landing techniques – techniques later used in Italy and Normandy.

On the naval front, however, there had been a number of British successes. *Gneisenau* was badly damaged by bombers, the *Tirpitz* was bottled-up in its Norwegian fiord and the German surface fleet had been effectively neutralized as a fighting force. Admiral Raeder found it necessary to resign; he was replaced by U-boat commander Karl Doenitz.

Where Raeder had been cautious, Doenitz was imaginative. His submariners were an élite, trained in the discomforts and terrors of living and working undersea – and they had already had a major impact on the war. Some of the latest U-boats were massive vessels with a range of up to 30,000 miles. The RAF, concerned primarily with bombing German cities, had not yet targeted German submarine pens as much as they

ABOVE AND BELOW: German U-boats under air attack from Britain's Coastal Command.

LEFT: A US Navy depth-charge attack. ABOVE: An American convoy escort in the Arctic.

might have. When the Americans found themselves at war, their shipping was badly hit by the wolf packs. In June 1942, the Allies lost another 700,000 tons of shipping; the figures continued to rise until March 1943, when a record number of U-boats were operating in the Atlantic.

But American merchant vessels were now mass-produced; each 'liberty ship' could be built in as little as four days. The Allies also used destroyer and corvette escorts to hit back at the wolf packs. Equipped with relatively sophisticated sonar devices and delayed action depth-charges, these were highly successful. In May 1943, for example, seven U-boats were sunk in a single night. Doenitz informed Hitler that the submarine campaign was in crisis, and withdrew his U-boats until new tactics could be developed.

In spite of the decisions taken at the Washington summit, throughout 1942 American and British service chiefs wrangled about what should be done next in Europe. The British were determined not to bow to Stalin's pressure and open a second front in Europe just yet; they convinced the Americans that it would fail without proper preparation and set the war effort back years. Even a bridgehead in Cherbourg was ruled out – unless the Russians looked in serious danger of defeat.

TITANIC STRUGGLE

The Battles for Stalingrad and Leningrad

At the beginning of 1942, General Zhukov's counter-attacks from Moscow and Leningrad began to peter out. Hitler's hopes rose again, and his general staff began to make plans for a new offensive. Renewed attacks would be made on Leningrad, but these would only form a diversion. Stalingrad in the south was to be the real objective. With this in their hands, the Germans could cut off central Russia from the Caucasus oilfields; and as the city bore the Soviet leader's name, it would be a tremendous propaganda coup.

The German commanders fought their usual internal battles over strategy, but their mood improved with news of the failure of two major

ABOVE: A German inspects a dead Russian tank. OPPOSITE: A soldier strides through wreckage outside Stalingrad.

Zhukov and his commanders.

Russian counter-attacks in the Crimea and near the Ukrainian city of Kharkov. In the latter case, the Southern Army under Semyon Timoshenko was all but annihilated. The Red Army also suffered a dent to their morale outside Leningrad when General Andrei Vlasov defected to the Germans with the intention of leading an anti-Soviet 'liberation' force.

On 28 June, 1942, the new German offensive began on either side of Kursk. "The Russian is finished," said Hitler, confidently dividing his forces in two. One army under General von Kleist headed south towards the oilfields, while the other under General Paulus struck towards Stalingrad – now being bombed massively from the air. As he moved his headquarters to the Ukraine to be nearer the seige, Hitler had no way of knowing that 24 August was to mark the limits of his conquests.

The Battle of Stalingrad has assumed mythic proportions in modern Russian history. It was a turning point in the war, but it was also a senseless slaughter caused chiefly by Hitler's refusal to contemplate any kind of withdrawal. Once inside the ruined, bombed-out city, the Germans lost their greatest advantage – mobility. They became locked in a vicious, attritional struggle for every foot of ground. The Russians had made every house a pill-box and every heap of rubble a strongpoint. As the casualty figures grew more atrocious each week, the German generals were forced to confront their perilous situation. But their warnings to Hitler were in vain. The Führer's will was unshakeable – "the last battalion will decide the issue," he said.

He had not predicted a Russian counter-offensive. In November, six Russian armies under Zhukov broke through lines held by Germans and Romanians north and south of Stalingrad. Four days later, they linked on the other side of the city, surrounding Paulus. The general's sensible suggestion of a tactical withdrawal was rejected by Hitler.

What could be done? Goering promised that his *Luftwaffe* would airdrop supplies, but appalling weather defeated this plan. General Manstein approached with a rescue force of

Timoshenko: successful resistance.

ABOVE: German artillery bombards Stalingrad. BELOW: German troops move to encircle Leningrad.

ABOVE AND BELOW: German bombardment devastated Stalingrad – but the Red Army used the rubble as defences.

ABOVE AND BELOW: Civilians managed a 'near-zero' existence among the ruins of Stalingrad.

ABOVE: Paulus pores over the maps. OPPOSITE: Stormtroopers move into Stalingrad.

Russian machine-gunners at the onset of winter, 1942.

ABOVE: A German soldier dug in, winter 1942.
LEFT: Russian artillery outside Stalingrad.
BELOW: A German supply column in trouble.

panzers but was halted 30 miles away. And still Hitler refused to contemplate a break-out.

By the new year it was too late anyway. Paulus, who mysteriously had just been promoted to field-marshal, surrendered on the 31 January, together with 24 generals and 91,000 German troops. Three days of mourning followed across Germany. "The god of war has gone over to the other side," said Hitler. But his commanders began to harbour serious doubts about his conduct of the war.

Two weeks later, the Russians had recaptured Kharkov – only to lose it again in March because the sacrifice of their Sixth Army had allowed the Germans time to regroup.

The Russian Front at this time witnessed some of the most appalling carnage in history. Both sides suffered from centralized control

General von Manstein.

exercised by remote dictators. Neither Hitler nor Stalin were prepared to accept withdrawals and this ideological rigidity exacted a terrible toll on human life. Time after time, thousands died in the pursuit of hopeless objectives or in the defence of hopeless positions. With its huge popula-

ABOVE: Soviet troops at Kursk, July 1943. OPPOSITE: A Russian T-34 tank in flames.

tion, however, Russia was better able to stand these losses. And the Germans had yet another disadvantage. Details of their plans were being decoded by the British and passed directly to Soviet command; so when Hitler's next great operation, Citadel, began in the summer of 1943 with nearly 2500 tanks and 900,000 men spread out across a 100-mile front, the Red Army was prepared for it.

The northern force under Feldmarshal Gunther von Kluge met fierce resistance straight away, though in the south SS troops under Manstein made some progress. The pivotal moment of the battle took place outside Kursk on 12 July, when 700 panzers under General Herman Hoth clashed with 850 T-34s under Marshal Pavel Rotmistrov. The panzers got the worst of it, and the following day a Russian counter-attack broke through the German lines, pushing them back 150 miles. The German losses were fearful: 70,000 men, 1400 planes and 1500 panzers. It marked the beginning of what was to become a long, agonizing retreat to Berlin.

DESERT STORM

The North African Campaign

Compared to the enormous death struggle of the Russian Front, the battles in North Africa were relatively small affairs. Nonetheless, for both Churchill and Hitler they had great strategic as well as symbolic importance.

The long siege of Tobruk and its heroic Australian garrison under General Leslie Morshead had carried on throughout the summer of 1941. Though the Australians received supplies from the Royal Navy, which ran the gauntlet of Italian submarines and German dive-bombers, by autumn that year their plight was becoming desperate. To lift the seige, the British launched Operation Crusader, targeting German panzers around Sidi Rezegh. It was generally successful; with only 40 tanks left

ABOVE: The *Afrika Korps* on the move. OPPOSITE: 'Desert Rats' clearing mines with bayonets.

intact, Rommel abandoned the area and Tobruk was relieved.

But in the early months of 1942, the German general began to claw back lost territory, and in May he launched a new offensive at Gazala. He was determined both to take Tobruk and forestall any new British offensive. The Tobruk garrison, now consisting of South African troops backed by British and Indian auxilianies, soon found itself under severe pressure. On 20 June 1942, Stukas and panzers made a combined assault on the city. Within three hours, its defences had been breached, and the following day the whole garrison of some 35,000 troops was forced to surrender. Apart from the fall of Singapore, this was probably the worst British defeat of the war. Hitler was so delighted that he promoted Rommel to field marshal.

LEFT AND BELOW: British 6-inch howitzers versus German 15cm guns.
BOTTOM: A German panzer crew outside Tobruk.

ABOVE: January 1942 – Rommel in Benghazi. **LEFT:** Australian troops in Tobruk.

Auchinleck pauses for thought in his Cairo HQ.

British troops attempt to shove a lorry out of the sand.

British PoWs leave Tobruk following the fall of the city.

Field Marshal Rommel pursued the British Eighth Army from Tobruk to Mersa Matruh, then on to El Alamein near the Egyptian border. Some of Rommel's advisors urged caution – but he was not a cautious man: he was often to be found right up on the front line in the midst of the battle, urging his soldiers on. "No admiral ever won a naval battle from the shore," he said.

The populations of Cairo and Alexandria braced themselves for the arrival of the *Afrika Korps*; Mussolini himself flew in to Libya, his white charger following in a plane behind, ready to enter Cairo in style. The British fleet sailed out of Alexandria and into the Red Sea. "Only 100 more miles to Alexandria," wrote Rommel to his wife on 30 June. But having advanced some 300 miles in a week, his troops were exhausted.

El Alamein was only 60 miles from Alexandria, but it was ideal terrain for defence, bounded by the sea to the north and the near-impassable Qattara Depression to the south. The first battle there began on 30 June 1942, and throughout July the Allies and Axis forces pushed each other

Australian troops writing home from 'heaven'.

Alexander: new regional commander, summer 1942.

backwards and forwards, with the Axis taking heavy losses.

Auchinleck's counter-attack on 21 July finally halted Rommel's advance – but did not do much more. Churchill flew out to Egypt on 4 August, weighing in his mind the pros and cons of changing the British command. In the event, he sacked Auchinleck and put General Sir Harold Alexander in his place as commander-in-chief. Churchill's first choice for the Eighth Army itself, General Gott, was killed in an air crash the next day. And so it was that General Sir Bernard Montgomery was flown out from England to take over the Eighth Army.

Both sides spent the rest of August creating defensive fortifications and minefields. Montgomery ignored repeated demands from Churchill to attack; he knew his supply routes were more secure than his opponent's, and calmly built up his strength. "If the attack begins in

Montgomery, wearing an Australian hat, arrives near El Alamein.

Americans and Free French had wrangled over the project for some time; the spectacular escape of French general Henri Giraud from a prisonor-of-war camp in Germany confused delicate negotiations between the local Vichy commanders and the American general Mark Clark, who had been put ashore by submarine to persuade them not to resist. In the event, the Giraud episode had little or no influence on Vichy forces, and the landings went largely unopposed.

The collaborationist press in Paris called for the Vichy government to declare war on the Allies, but Pétain equivocated, telling his deputy in North Africa, Admiral Jean Darlan, to take whatever action he saw fit.

Hitler was furious, and chose this moment to end his arrangement with Pétain: German troops marched into southern France. In response, the Vichy French scuttled their own fleet which was anchored at Toulon and Darlan decided to co-operate with the Allies. He was made high commissioner in North Africa, but was assassinated shortly afterwards by a French royalist.

In early 1943, heavily outnumbered and short of supplies, Rommel continued to use an audacious series of counter-attacks to dent Allied morale in Western Libya and Tunisia. The new Anglo-American command structure was easily confused. "I think the best way to describe our operations to date is that they have violated every recognized principle

LEFT AND ABOVE: American troops come ashore in Tunisia.

Eisenhower at his headquarters.

Italian prisoners in Tunisia, spring 1943.

ABOVE: Free French troops enter Tunis. BELOW: End of the line – a German PoW under US guard.

of war, are in conflict with all operational and logistic methods laid down in text books, and will be condemned in their entirety by all Leavenworth and War College classes for the next 25 years," wrote the Allied commander, General Dwight D. Eisenhower.

These temporary reverses ruled out any imminent Allied landing in northern Europe. Historians argue that this was a blessing in disguise: it encouraged the German commander-in-chief Albrecht von Kesselring to pour reinforcements into Tunisia, which were not then available to oppose the Allies when they came to invade Sicily later that year.

Fortunately, the Axis armies had almost exhausted their oil supplies and the Allies possessed overwhelming superiority in terms of military hardware and firepower. A German counter-offensive in March proved abortive – causing Rommel to leave Africa for good. On 8 May the Allies entered Tunis, taking 130,000 Axis prisoners. "We are masters of the North African shore," General Alexander reported to Churchill.

BOMBING THE CITIES

The Air War over Europe

In 1941, the British bombing offensive over Germany was still comparatively small. No matter that precision bombing proved impossible at night, and that daylight bombing was impossible without fighter cover; no matter that initially more aircrew were lost than Germans killed: bombing was seen as one of the few ways in which Britain could strike back at the enemy and, despite the lessons of the Blitz, Bomber Command believed the air raids would weaken German morale. Night after night, RAF Wellingtons and Halifaxes made the hazardous journey across the North Sea and through a storm of flak to drop their payloads on German cities.

An RAF Wellington bomber and crew.

US B-17 Flying Fortresses over Germany.

In November 1941, a temporary halt to the offensive was ordered, but the dream of bombing Germany into submission remained. Enormous industrial resources in Britain and America were devoted to the strategy, while other more pressing needs, such as fighting the U-boat war in the Atlantic, were sidelined.

By early 1942, British bombers had been fitted with radio directional equipment to help them find more specific targets. But a directive issued on Valentine's Day emphasized that the new bombing policy was aimed not at undermining German industrial capacity *per se*, but at destroying the morale of industrial workers.

Sir Arthur Harris, who had studied the methods adopted by the *Luftwaffe* during the Blitz, was put in charge of Bomber Command a few days later. He and his American counterparts now based in British airfields devised their own strategies, sure they could win the war from the air. Harris began his tenure by ordering an incendiary raid on the historic town of Lubeck. "Lubeck was not a vital target," said Harris later. "But it seemed to me better to destroy an industrial town of moderate importance than to toil to destroy a large industrial city." Some 15,000 civilians lost their homes.

Bomb-loaders and mechanics work on a Wellington.

B-17s on a daylight bombing raid.

Lubeck was followed by four raids on Rostock in April. In May, the first 1000-bomber raid was mounted, with Cologne as its target. Forty bombers were downed and, unknown to the British public, the city was operating normally again within two weeks. Harris knew the raids were ineffective, but argued that they were good practice for later raids, and the myth of faltering morale in the German cities drove him and his political masters to devote even more effort and lives to the project. By the summer of 1942, improved German air defences meant that Bomber

Command was losing an average of three and half per cent of planes on every mission.

At the Casablanca conference, Roosevelt and Churchill agreed on round-the-clock bombing of Axis targets – the new British Lancasters flying by night and the American B-17 Flying Fortresses by day. Berlin was the target of 50,000 tons of bombs in 1943 alone. But when the strategic bombing raids were at their height, so was German industrial production, spurred on by Hitler's architect Albert Speer, now Nazi minister in charge of war production.

At this stage, then, the raids were having small impact on Germany's industrial base. The exception was a series of bold RAF strikes at the industrial Ruhr from March to July 1943 – the so-called Dambusters' raids in which the specially-trained 617 Squadron used Dr Barnes Wallis's experimental 'bouncing bombs' to breach three major dams and flood the valleys below. Eight of the 19 bombers taking part in the mission were lost.

After July, the port of Hamburg became the Allies' major target, suffering 33 raids. The biggest, known as Operation Gomorrah, took place in the early hours of 28 July. Though the raid lasted only 43 minutes, the

TOP: Air Chief Marshall Sir Arthur Harris. ABOVE: Air crews attend a briefing.

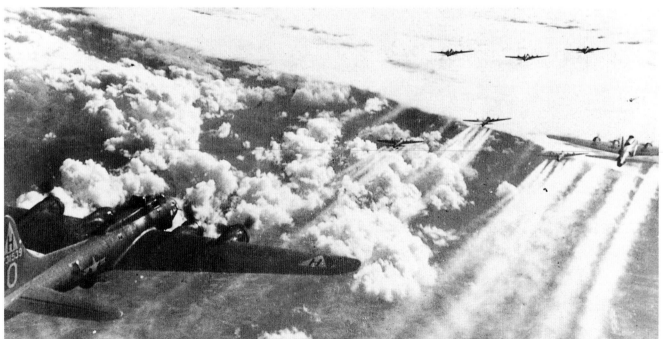

Formation-flying B-17s brave flak and fighter attack to deliver their payloads.

Dr Barnes Wallis – inventor of the bouncing bomb.

combination of incendiary bombs and tinder-dry conditions produced a firestorm which burned out eight square miles of the city and killed 42,000 people – more than the number of British casualties for the whole of the Blitz. Nonetheless, the city's factories were back in production within a few weeks.

From November 1943, attention shifted to Berlin, pleasing Stalin and relieving Churchill of Soviet pressure for an immediate second front. Losses were now running at over five per cent, however, and Bomber Command's morale was being sapped; the American Eighth Airforce sustained still greater losses.

The military effectiveness of the bombing campaign was now being questioned by Harris's superiors, and its morality by churchmen – notably by the Bishop of Chichester, George Bell, who lost his chance of being Archbishop of Canterbury as a result. Even Churchill had his doubts. "Are we beasts?" he asked after seeing a film of bombing from the air. "Are we taking this too far?"

By early 1944, Harris was having to ask for night-fighter support for his bombers. The Eighth Air Force was already using its new long-range fighter, the Mustang, for this task, and had now shifted its daylight attacks on to German synthetic oil and ball-bearing plants – seriously delaying the development and introduction of the new German jet aircraft and long-range submarines.

Top and Above: The destruction of Cologne, targeted by both British and American bombers.

German homeless prepare to leave Cologne.

In preparation for a future second front, both British and Americans bombing raids concentrated on destroying German transport in France. The danger here, as Churchill saw it, was that indiscriminate bombing would alienate the French population: the missions simply had to be accurate. But despite meticulous planning, many bombs went wide of the mark. In April 1943, as many as 228 French civilians were killed in an American raid on the Renault factory outside Paris, while another USAAF attack on an aircraft factory near Antwerp killed nearly 1000 civilians, including 236 schoolchildren.

ABOVE: The ruins of Berlin. BELOW: The Daimler-Benz factory following a raid.

ABOVE: German AA guns. ABOVE RIGHT: Notching up missions on a Liberator. BELOW: A B-17 hit by flak.

The Renault works at Billancourt after the Allied raid.

The raids on German cities did succeed in removing German air defences from the Russian front; but with the benefit of hindsight, it appears that saturation or 'terror' bombing had mainly negative strategic consequences. As civilians cowered in their shelters under the thunder of the bombs, their resolve did not collapse like the buildings outside. Far from it. Witnessing the deaths of innocents – old people, women and children – only hardened the hatred of the populace for the Allied raiders in the skies. The Nazi propaganda machine was thus handed victory upon victory.

'THE SOFT UNDERBELLY'

Allied Landings in the Mediterranean

Ever since he had contemplated military strategy as First Lord of the Admiralty during the Great War, Churchill had believed that Europe was vulnerable to attack from the south. The belief had led him into the disastrous Gallipoli campaign of 1915, just as it had led him to shore up Greek defences in 1941. In May 1943, as he pored over the maps in Washington with the joint chiefs of staff, he once again urged a Mediterranean operation – namely the invasion of Italy via Sicily and of northern Europe via Austria.

Italy's war effort had already been seriously undermined; little remained of Mussolini's military strength and with the conquest of North Africa, the Mediterranean was once again open to Allied convoys. When the Japanese ambassador went to see Mussolini in 1942, all he could say

ABOVE: A US amphibious DUKW, or 'duck', comes ashore in Sicily. OPPOSITE: British troops wait to land.

ABOVE: British Sherman tanks loaded for the beaches.
BELOW: An American cargo ship is hit by dive-bombers.

to him was: "You, Duce, you worn out, very worn out, too worn out."

It was at this point that the 'Man Who Never Was' – a corpse dressed as a British officer and bearing fake documents implying that the Allied invasion was planned for Greece and Sardinia – was washed up in Spain, and may have succeeded in duping Nazi intelligence. Whether or not this was so, on 10 July 1943 Montgomery's force of nearly half a million men landed in Sicily almost unopposed. The Americans, however, faced stiffer resistance. At the same time, a feud developed between Montgomery and the headstrong American general, George Patton, over strategy. So there was some delay before Allied forces managed to take Palermo and Messina in August and, in a kind of mini-Dunkirk carried out in 70 small naval vessels and 50 rubber boats, many Axis troops managed to escape to the mainland with their equipment.

Hitler and Mussolini had met on 19 July; Mussolini was ill and barely spoke. He faced not simply invasion but economic collapse – Turin and

Ships burning in the Sicilian port of Palermo.

General Patton gives orders in Sicily.

American howitzers bombard retreating Axis troops.

ABOVE: Sicilian partisans. OPPOSITE: A US soldier poses in Brolo, Sicily.

Kesselring discusses his Italian defences.

Milan were in the grip of major strikes. Less than a week later, King Victor Emanuel III dismissed him from office and installed Marshal Pietro Badoglio in his place. Mussolini was smuggled out of the palace and then taken by ambulance to the island of Pozna "for his own safety". Almost overnight, fascism disappeared from Italy.

Hitler was deeply concerned: a conversation between Roosevelt and Churchill discussing the terms for Italy's surrender had been intercepted by his agents. Rommel was sent to the Alpine passes and Kesselring was given reinforcements in southern Italy. By the beginning of September, the Germans were deeply entrenched. On 8 September, the Allies unexpectedly announced the 'surrender' of Italian forces – even though the Italians had still received no orders to that effect. At the same time, a massive Allied landing force was steaming towards the beaches of Salerno.

The fate of Italian troops was unenviable. They were disarmed by their former allies, who treated them as no better than turncoats. In Cephalonia in Greece over 1600 Italian soldiers were slaughtered by the

Salerno under bombardment by US warships.

British Bren-carriers come ashore near Salerno.

US general Mark Clark on the Salerno beach-head.

Naples under air attack.

SS; another 3000 Italians, sent back to Germany for forced labour, were drowned when their ship was torpedoed by the Allies. By the end of September 1943, 100,000 Italian soldiers in Greece had been sent to labour camps in Germany, and Badoglio and the Italian king had been forced to flee to Bari. Only the remainder of the Italian fleet managed to escape, sailing to join the British in Malta.

At midnight on 9 September, the US Fifth Army under Clark began to land at Salerno, opposed by six of Kesselring's divisions. Resistance was at first so fierce that the operation nearly ended in evacuation. The new German guided bombs disabled the British battleship *Warspite*, which had been supporting the landings, and sank the Italian battleship *Roma* (now on the Allied side); Kesselring's forces also succeeded in capturing the Italian naval port of Taranto.

Other Mediterranean landings met with more immediate success. The Germans withdrew from Corsica ahead of the Free French, while American troops took Capri. But German reinforcements on the Greek island of Rhodes forestalled a British landing there.

On 12 September, German paratroopers rescued an exhausted Mussolini from the mountain Gran Sasso, where he was being kept by Italian police. He was flown to meet Hitler, and proclaimed a new fascist

ABOVE: Unloading supplies at Anzio. BELOW: US trucks and bulldozers come ashore at Anzio.

republic in German-occupied northern Italy. He was to be given some reason to hope that the Germans might prove victorious in his country. Though the Allies took Naples on 1 October, from this point until the end of 1943 they managed to advance only 70 miles. "The stagnation of the whole campaign on the Italian front is becoming scandalous," stormed Churchill. Kesselring, who had been expecting an attack on Rome by air and sea – which might have forced him to abandon the south – was given the chance to build up his defences.

There was worse news to come for the Allies. Their delays convinced Hitler to reinforce Kesselring, but they were also making decisions with serious long-term implications. The Americans in southern Italy had rearmed the Mafia, rooted out by the fascists (it remains powerful there to this day). An Italian resistance group in Rome was campaigning for the king to be overthrown as well, and the Russians were refused a place

TOP AND ABOVE: American machine-gunners outside Anzio.

Monte Cassino before its destruction.

on the Anglo-American Control Commission for occupied Italy – setting a dangerous precedent for the control of Eastern Europe after the war.

Another operator who made effective use of the Italian surrender was Josip Broz Tito, the successful Yugoslav Communist leader, who disarmed Italian troops and took their equipment. Tito and the army colonel Draza Mihailovic now controlled 250,000 men and were keeping eight German divisions pinned down in Yugoslavia. Churchill, advised by his son Randolph, was backing Tito because he was more active. The Americans and, strangely, Stalin, were still backing Mihailovic.

Meanwhile, the American Fifth Army was crawling up the west of Italy while the British Eighth Army, now under the command of Sir Oliver Leese, crawled up the east. They were certainly taking their time. Through the early months of 1944, the Allies were obstructed by the German fortifications, the 'Gustav Line', south of Rome. A successful landing at Anzio on 22 January looked set to break the deadlock (only 13 soldiers were killed coming ashore) but once again Allied generals were indecisive, and soon the whole offensive was threatened as Kesselring rushed reinforcements to the area.

In the centre of the Allied advance lay the ancient monastery

A British soldier in the ruins of Monte Cassino.

ABOVE: A British mortar battery in action. BELOW: Bombardment in the Monte Cassino area.

ABOVE: British stretcher-bearers rescue the wounded at Cassino. BELOW: The monastery after the surrender of German troops.

New Zealanders with German prisoners, Cassino.

of Monte Cassino, which Alexander believed had been fortified by the Germans. On 13 February, 400 tons of bombs were dropped on the monastery, reducing it to rubble. The Germans, who had held back from entering the monastery, were now prepared to use the ruins to intensify their defence. In three attacks the Allies suffered grievous losses. The strongpoint was finally taken in May 1944, when the Polish Corps took the brunt of the German response while Free French troops under General Juin managed to sneak through the mountains behind.

But Allied confusion again delayed the advance up Italy. Determined to reach Rome first (which he did on 4 June), Clark allowed the retreating Germans to reinforce another defensive line further north of the capital.

The Italian campaign was demoralizing from the Allied point of view: at every river, every range

Badoglio in Brindisi.

Allied landings south of Rome, January 1944.

of hills, they faced a string of skilled German rearguard actions. The desertion rate increased.

By the end of the 1944, however, Canadian forces had taken Ravenna – though they had not yet reached Bologna or the Valley of the Po as they had intended – ready for their drive north into Austria. But a German counter-attack on 26 December, and the removal of another five Allied divisions to the Western Front, forced the British and Americans to go on the defensive and sit tight until spring 1945.

Mark Clark arrives in the 'open city' of Rome.

RESISTANCE AND COLLABORATION

Partisans and Puppet Régimes in Occupied Europe

By the end of 1941, the whole of Europe from the outskirts of Moscow to the Pyrenees and from Crete to the Arctic Circle was, with the exception of neutral Sweden and Switzerland, in Nazi hands. The treatment of conquered peoples was always cruel, but just how cruel depended entirely on their ethnic origins.

The Nazis regarded all Slavs as subhuman, for example. In spite of propaganda talk of 'liberating' the Russians from Communism, the Nazis were only interested in exploiting Slavic peoples. "Whether they thrive or starve to death concerns me only from the point of view of our need for

French resistance fighters in Bordeaux.

Himmler visits the concentration camp at Dachau.

them as slave labour for our own civilisation," said SS chief Heinrich Himmler. "In all other respects I am totally indifferent."

The Danes, Norwegians and Dutch, on the other hand, were considered to be Germanic. Norway and Holland were put under the control of civilian commissars, while in Denmark Hitler only demanded his own nominee as prime minister after the Danish king had failed to reply to congratulations on his 72nd birthday.

A Vichy-run prison camp in southern France.

In most occupied countries there was little local support for the Nazis. Norwegian and Dutch fascists like Quisling and Anton Mussert were given power, but they were deeply unpopular; even Hitler regarded them with contempt (he described Quisling as "a blown-up rubber pig which emits a loud squeaking noise and then collapses").

Some local fascists were also prepared to back the Gestapo or join the SS, but these were generally few and far between. At the end of the war, these men were either captured and put on trial or, like the French fascist leader Marcel Deat, they simply disappeared.

But the Germans needed collaborators to make the occupation work. This posed hard questions for ordinary people, who had to decide exactly where 'normal' life ended and collaboration began. Joining the notorious *Milice* in France was clearly collaboration; having day-to-day business dealings with Germans was less obviously wrong. And then there were the local women who consorted with German soldiers. It was a time of moral darkness, in which individuals had to grope their way forward as best they could. Nonetheless, as it became clear that the Germans might not win the war after all, occupied peoples turned increasingly to different forms of resistance.

Resistance saboteurs inspect the wreckage of a train in the French Alps.

A Resistance 'ambulance' ferries the wounded from 'the front line'.

Parading a Danish collaborator through the streets.

May 1942: Heydrich's car after the attempt on his life in Prague.

To start with, resistance took the form of symbolic gestures or civil disobedience. Slogans were daubed on walls, while the vast majority of Norwegians refused to play sports because they did not want to be associated with the Nazi sports administration. The churches were often in the forefront of non-violent protest. All Norwegian bishops 'resigned' after police stopped crowds listening to an anti-Quisling sermon at Trondheim Cathedral, and the Belgian primate Cardinal van Roey judged that it was "wrong for Catholics to collaborate in the establishment of a tyrannical régime. Indeed they are under an obligation to work with those who resist such a régime." Later in the war, the sacrament was denied members of the Nazi police in Belgium. The Belgian fascist leader Leon Degrelle was even excommunicated in 1943 following a punch-up with his local dean.

"The Jews have got to be got out of Europe, if necessary by applying the most brutal methods," Goebbels told his diary in March 1942. "No other government and no other régime would have the strength for such a global solution as this." Sometimes non-co-operation took

Victims of the SS, Oradour-sur-Glane.

ABOVE AND RIGHT: The dynamiting of Lidice, Czechoslovakia, in revenge for Heydrich's assassination (before, during and aft

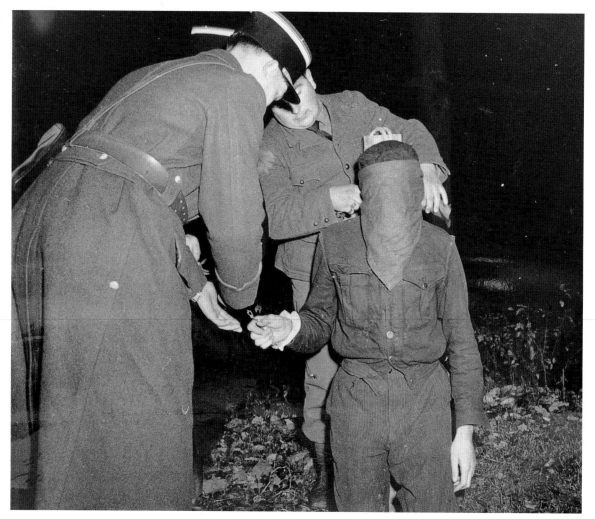

A collaborator is blindfolded before execution, France.

place *because* of the Nazi 'final solution'. In February 1941, there was a mass strike in Holland following the arrest of Jews, while the Danish king threatened to abdicate if anti-semitic legislation was introduced in his country. In Croatia, the Archbishop of Zagreb demanded that the collaborationist government confirm the rumours of deportation. And after the BBC revealed the fate of 700,000 Polish Jews in a broadcast in June 1942, there was resistance even in Germany: the churchmen Karl Friedrich Stellbrink and Dietrich Bonhoeffer were arrested and later

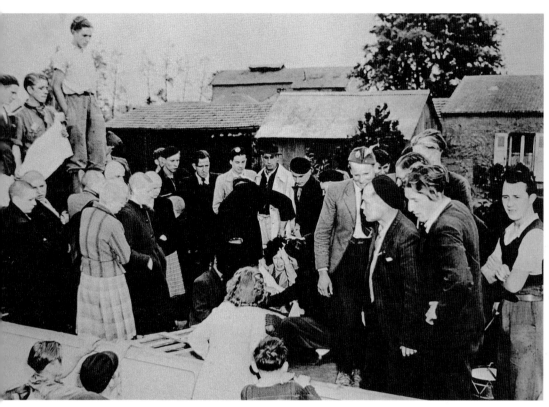

French women have their heads shaved for 'consorting with the enemy'.

executed for their outspoken condemnation of the régime.

Then there was the underground news, gleaned from the BBC European Service and from Swiss radio. Up to 12,000 Belgians were involved in producing 300 underground newspapers – the first ones being published the day after Belgian forces surrendered. In France at least 1000 underground papers and pamphlets were published during the occupation; while the Danish underground newspapers had a circulation of 10 million. Even in Germany, an estimated 10 million people listened to the BBC towards the end of the war – though the punishment for doing so was death.

If there was a single Nazi policy that encouraged resistance, however, it was the conscription of workers for German factories. Many young people preferred to go underground where they learned to make explosives from stolen chemicals or equipment airdropped by the British and Americans. In Britain itself, resistance agents were trained in special schools and routes in and out of Europe were developed for resistance leaders or escaping Allied airmen. Thousands of European civilians took enormous risks to help with acts of subversion.

Outright resistance or sabotage needed great courage: anyone caught faced certain death, and brutal 'examples' were made of the innocent. Such reprisals became increasingly savage as the war went on. In France, General Wilhelm Keitel (later hanged as a war criminal) used his infamous 'Night and Fog' order to set out a reprisal rate of 100 civilian deaths for every German killed, and 50 for every German wounded: by the end of the war at least 30,000 French hostages had been shot. In May 1942, following the assassination of the brutal Nazi ruler of German-occupied Czechoslovakia, Reinhard Heydrich, the village of Lidice was dynamited and everyone in it murdered or deported as a 'lesson'. Other victims included

Secret caves used by the Dutch resistance.

French Resistance fighters clean their weapons and receive medical attention.

642 inhabitants of the French village of Oradour-sur-Glane, massacred by an SS unit following the Normandy landings in 1944.

By early 1944, some resistance groups were tempted into outright battles with the Germans. Over 4000 men of the Forces Françaises de l'Interieur (FFI), for example, fought for a week at Montmouchet before being overwhelmed. Another section rose up at Vercors, near Grenoble, in the tragically mistaken belief that an Allied air landing was imminent. Despite such disasters, by June that year the French Resistance could provide the Allies with the equivalent of almost 15 divisions behind enemy lines. In the months that followed, they would hunt down the last remnants of the Nazi régime and take summary vengeance on many of those who had collaborated with it.

LIBERATION

THE ALLIES ADVANCE ON ALL FRONTS

D-DAY

The Normandy Landings

In November 1943, Stalin finally agreed to meet Roosevelt and Churchill at Tehran. Roosevelt was determined to reach agreement with the Russians – even if it meant alienating his old friend Churchill. The conference began uneasily; Churchill had completely lost his voice, and was forced to listen while Stalin roundly criticized Chiang Kai-shek and Roosevelt attacked de Gaulle. Roosevelt then asked Stalin how he thought the Germans could be defeated rapidly, and without a moment's thought the Soviet leader replied that an Allied landing had to be made in northern France. Churchill managed to voice his disquiet: the failure of such a project would have terrible consequences. Eventually Roosevelt

Allied troops training in England before D-Day.

American troops dash ashore, Normandy 6 June 1944.

managed to persuade him that its success would shorten the war by years.

For the next six months or so, Operation Overlord was planned in meticulous detail in London and Washington, while enormous forces were gathered in southern England – 10,000 aircraft, over 4000 landing craft, and 1500 warships. Eisenhower was made supreme commander.

But a number of disputes over strategy had to be resolved before the operation could go ahead. American commanders rejected de Gaulle's idea of using the French Resistance as an alternative to air raids on the German transport system in France and Belgium. This led to outrage among the French, who were to lose as many as 3000 civilians in just one 48-hour period at the end of May 1944. But by then the French railways

Eisenhower: Allied supreme commander.

Reconnaissance view of the Cherbourg beach before D-Day.

A US Marauder returns from a bombing mission over Normandy.

US gliders on the Cherbourg peninsula.

were all but destroyed, as were most of the Seine and Loire bridges.

Then the Allied faced the problem of where to land. The Pas de Calais was nearest, while Normandy was less heavily defended. Normandy was finally agreed on, as intelligence indicated that the Germans were convinced of a Calais beach-head. To make sure the Germans remained convinced of it, Calais was bombed heavily and a fictitious army group under the 'command' of General Patton was set up in Kent. In fact, the German generals were divided on the subject. Von Rundstedt, the com-

ABOVE: RAF Air Marshal Tedder.
RIGHT: US transports cross the Channel.
BELOW: American paratroopers.

Omaha beach: supplies pour off the transport ships.

mander in chief in western Europe, believed the landings would be at the Pas de Calais; Rommel, in charge of shore defences, believed it would be Normandy. Because of this dispute, German forces had to be divided between the two. As 5 June, D-Day, approached, the Germans were also given a false sense of security by a storm raging in the Channel; Rommel was even away with his wife in Germany.

In fact, the foul weather delayed the invasion for 24 hours. On the night of 5 June, the wind suddenly dropped. At 9.30pm a secret message was broadcast by the BBC which gave the go-ahead for the French Resistance to cut more railway lines across the country. Nearly 1000 successful attacks took place, though in the days that followed the SS would take a terrible revenge on villages suspected of involvement. At 11.55 pm,

ABOVE AND OPPOSITE: **Establishing the beach-heads, Normandy.**

Tending the wounded on Omaha Beach.

US troops take the cliffs above Omaha beach.

The first German PoWs in Normandy.

The liberation of Cherbourg.

the first British paratroopers landed six miles north of Caen – and the invasion had begun.

By the end of the following day, an enormous fleet of landing craft had managed to put 156,000 men ashore on five Normandy beaches, with one exception under lighter German fire than expected. Even so, there were serious traffic snarl-ups and many soldiers drowned after their landing craft were flooded by the heavy seas. And there were other set-backs. The British and Canadians failed to take Caen on the first day (it took a month and the medieval town was flattened in the process), while the Americans missed one of their beaches and the capture of

ABOVE: The battle for Caen. RIGHT: Canadian troops move through the ruins of Caen.

The aftermath of a firefight on one of the roads in Normandy.

July 1944: Hitler inspects the bunker after the attempt on his life.

Cherbourg was seriously delayed. Then from 19 to 22 June, the advance from the beach-heads was hampered by one of the worst storms in Europe for 40 years.

But in general Operation Overlord was a staggering success. Once the landings had been consolidated, the Allied commanders knew that it would be next to impossible for the Germans to dislodge their forces from Northern France. On the other hand, the German response was confused. "What should we do?" Von Runstedt was asked. "End the war! What else!" he replied. Hitler dismissed him for defeatism.

Rommel was also suddenly removed from command while recovering from injuries sustained when his staff car was strafed by an Allied fighter. He had been involved in Colonel von Stauffenberg's heroic attempt to assassinate Hitler on 20 July: but the bomb only succeeded in injuring Hitler. Rommel was offered the

Judge Friesler sentences the July plotters.

ABOVE: Churchill watches the landings in southern France (see below) from the British destroyer *Kimberley.*

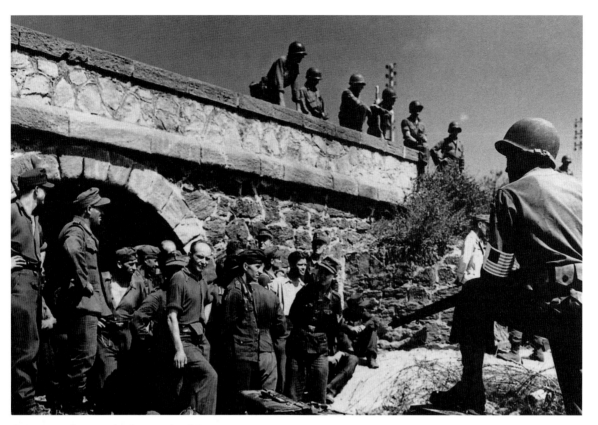

German prisoners in the south of France.

The liberation of Aix.

228

August 1944: Parisians rise up against the occupiers.

choice between suicide and the 'People's Court'; he chose suicide.

In Normandy the Allies twice allowed a large number of German divisions to slip through the net – though some 50,000 PoWs were taken. Feldmarshal von Kluge was accused of trying to negotiate the surrender of his own forces when he was recalled to Berlin; he committed suicide rather than face Hitler's wrath. On his body was a note which read, "The German people have suffered such unspeakable ills, that the time has come to put an end to these horrors."

Parts of northern France were now liberated: the time had come for an Allied landing in the south. Operation Anvil took place on 15 August, with 50,000 Allied troops landing on the Côte D'Azur. On the same day, Eisenhower's plans to bypass Paris altogether were scuppered by a resistance uprising in the city. De Gaulle ignored the supreme commander's express instructions and ordered the French Second Armoured Division under General Leclerc to liberate the city. Unsure what to do, Leclerc sent a detachment ahead with orders to mix with American troops if they

Paris: Resistance fighters take cover from German sniper-fire.

had got to the suburbs first. Eisenhower relented – just as a temporary ceasefire between the German commandant, General Dietrich von Cholditz, and the local Resistance expired. "Paris is not to fall into the hands of the enemy, except as a heap of rubble," signalled Hitler to the dismayed von Cholditz.

But the Francophile von Cholditz had no intention of destroying Paris, and he surrendered when Leclerc's forces arrived on 25 August. Just then the news broke that SS soldiers had broken into Marshal Pétain's hotel room and taken him as a virtual prisoner to Belfort. Pétain had been planning to go to Paris himself and renounce the Armistice; his abduction cleared the way for General de Gaulle, who proclaimed himself President of France from the steps of the Hôtel de Ville in Paris. There followed a jubilant ceremonial parade through the streets, despite the danger from a few remaining German snipers. By the end of 26 August 1944, after four years of brutal oppression, the City of Light was once again free.

De Gaulle, Leclerc and Juin in Paris.

Parisians begin the Liberation party.

Paris crowds surge round de Gaulle's car.

THE RED TIDE

The Advance of Stalin's Armies

Since the Battle of Kursk in the summer of 1943, the Red Army had been advancing steadily to the Russian border. But it was a slow, bloody process: resistance was fierce everywhere and not once did the German lines collapse.

General Zhukov's infantry were on the whole untrained and short of supplies; they lived on whatever they could loot or 'liberate' during the advance. "Russian soldiers carry their sacks on their backs full of dry crusts of bread and raw vegetables collected on the march from the fields and villages," reported one German commander. "The horses eat the

Russians break through German defences outside Leningrad.

ABOVE AND BELOW: The Ukrainian town of Zhitomir is torched by retreating Germans.

ABOVE AND BELOW: T-34s advance through the snow in the East.

Red Army troops rush across a field near the Vistula River in the Ukraine.

The Russian general, Nikolai Vatutin.

Polish bodies uncovered at Katyn, April 1943.

T-34s advance near Lvov.

straw from the house roofs – they get very little else." Red Army troops were also, it seemed, expendable: Zhukov's method of clearing enemy minefields was simply to march them across them. In the Great Patriotic War, as Stalin called it, up to 90 per cent of all young Russian men between the ages of 18 and 21 were killed in action.

But nothing but bad news came to the Wolf's Lair from the Russian Front. Hitler was forced into the forlorn hope that the alliance drawn up against him would collapse. There were, of course, areas of conflict between Stalin, Roosevelt and Churchill. One was the future of Poland. In April 1943, the Germans discovered the bodies of 4000 murdered Polish officers at Katyn: it seemed likely that Stalin's secret police had committed the atrocity. The Polish government in exile was outraged. Plainly, once the Nazis had been defeated in Poland, it was going to be impossible to reconcile the aims of legitimate Polish leaders with those of the Red Army. Roosevelt had to urge an angry Churchill to keep his counsel in the interests of the alliance.

In January 1944, when Leningrad was finally relieved, the Russian advance began to accelerate. In March, the Red Army entered Romania and by the end of May it had cleared the Crimea and recovered nearly all Soviet territory. In late June, to coincide with the second front in France, up to 160 Soviet divisions hit the German strongpoint around Minsk; within a week, 350,000 German prisoners had been taken and the German lines were at last in tatters. The Russian armies poured through the breach, swinging west into Poland. On 1 August, they halted on the outskirts of Warsaw.

There then followed one of those tragic episodes of the war, of raised hopes and betrayal, which did so much to undermine relations between East and West. The Poles in London intended to follow de Gaulle's example in Paris and liberate their own capital city; they saw the arrival

Soviet forces cross a Polish river.

Russians attack German troops in a farmhouse near Lvov.

Russians advance along the coast in Lithuania.

Russian self-propelled guns move through a forest in the Baltic.

The Red Army on the outskirts of Warsaw.

of Soviet troops in the Warsaw suburbs as the signal for a revolt in the city by the underground 'Home Army'.

Unfortunately for the Polish commander Bor-Komorowski, the Russians were told to stay where they were. It is probable that the order came directly from Stalin, who – with a cynical eye on the post-war world order – wanted Polish resistance to be destroyed before he took over the country. He used as an excuse the fact that three new German divisions had been called up to defend the city under the capable command of Walther Model.

The British and Americans protested. Stalin would not even allow Soviet airfields to be used to airlift supplies to the beleaguered Polish fighters, pressed on all sides by units of the SS. "Such intransigence", Churchill informed Stalin, "seems … at variance with the spirit of Allied co-operation to which you and we attach so much importance both for the present and for the future."

ABOVE: Polish snipers during the Warsaw Uprising. BELOW: The Polish underground army.

The Russian leader finally agreed to allow airdrops for the Poles on 9 September, and over 300 Allied sorties were flown over Warsaw by Polish, British, American and South African flyers. But he cashiered those Polish generals in the Red Army who tried to make contact with the insurgents in the Warsaw suburb of Czernakow, and at the beginning of October he once again vetoed any Allied use of Soviet airfields.

The consequences were terrible for the Poles in the honeycomb of the Warsaw ghetto: 15,000 fighters were killed and about 200,000 civilians murdered in reprisals following the uprising. The episode marked the effective beginning of 'cold' relations between East and West.

In Slovakia, an uprising by Communists was also brutally crushed by the Nazis. Other countries, however, had been more circumspect, and waited for Russian intentions to be clearly signalled before taking action against the Germans. On 23 August, knowing it was too late for Hitler to

Above: A German flame-thrower torches a Warsaw building, turning the Ghetto (opposite) into an inferno.

The Polish Home Army in action.

German officers discuss tactics in Warsaw.

US pontoon bridges waiting to be constructed across the Rhine.

US Army crossed the Meuse at Verdun on 31 August; four days later, on the fifth anniversary of Britain's declaration of war, the British Guards Armoured Division raced 75 miles through Belgium and into Brussels. More British tanks pressed on towards Antwerp, while Belgian paratroop commandos were dropped to help the Belgian resistance. By 10 September, the Americans were in control of the Belgian fort of Eben-Emael, which had played such a crucial role in the invasion in 1940. Two days later, Le Havre surrendered to the Allies.

But the Allied advance, at the limits of its supply lines, petered out before reaching Antwerp. "My men can eat their belts, but my tanks have

ABOVE: Hitler Youth members as young as 13 saw action. ABOVE RIGHT: German PoWs in Belgium.

gotta have gas," Patton shouted at Eisenhower when his tanks ran out of petrol on 31 August.

Other Allied tempers were short as well, as Montgomery and the American general Bradley battled over tactics. Eisenhower attempted to pacify them all. An ambitious attempt to press on through Holland and into Germany, known as Operation Market Garden, ended in disaster as British and Commonwealth paratroopers tried to secure the bridge over the Rhine at Arnhem. But they were dropped almost on top of two German armoured divisions. Lightly armed as they were, they could not resist the onslaught of the panzers for long, and thousands were taken prisoner.

The failure of Market Garden had serious consequences. The Dutch government in exile had called a railway strike to help the operation, and this led the Germans to exact brutal reprisals and fortify the northern part of the country. During that cold winter, some 15,000 Dutch people died of starvation; the rest kept themselves alive on a diet of sugar beet and tulip bulbs. An opportunity to end the war quickly was also lost. If

ABOVE: Camouflaging a US tank in Luxembourg. **BELOW:** Belt-feeding a snow-covered gun in Belgium.

ABOVE: British paratroopers make the drop over Arnhem.

Arnhem bridge following the failure of Operation Market Garden.

Wounded British troops surrender at Arnhem.

Entrenched British troops scan the woods near Arnhem.

The synthetic oil plant at Zeitz after an air raid.

the Allies had been prepared to support the Arnhem operation fully (many commanders profoundly disagreed with it), they might have been able to make a breakthrough in southern Germany and thousands of lives could have been saved; both East Berlin and Prague could also have been secured for democracy.

As things stood, the Allies did have a number of crucial advantages over their opponents. With the benefit of the Enigma code-breaking machines, they were reading signals almost at will, and one such told them that the *Luftwaffe* was running short of fuel. As a result, Allied bombing raids were now directed at German synthetic oil plants and fuel dumps. They also hit the flying bomb bases – of serious cause of concern to the British, Belgians and Dutch. As many as 2,754 V1s had already been launched at Britain, for example, and 2,752 people killed – almost one casualty per bomb – and this was nothing to the potential destructive power of the 11-ton V2 rockets. In October and November 1944, V2s were directed at the now-liberated city of Antwerp, with devastating results: nearly 4000 civilians and 700 Allied soldiers were killed.

By November 1944, most of France, Belgium and Greece had been liberated, the German border had been crossed at Aachen, and over two

A V2 rocket is launched.

The V2 experimental area after an air raid.

million Allied soldiers were in western Europe. Eisenhower had taken over from Montgomery as supreme commander of land forces.

In Quebec, Churchill was trying to persuade Roosevelt to take a united position on the future of Europe; but Roosevelt, about to face his fourth presidential election campaign, ignored his overtures. They could decide only that Germany should be de-industrialized after the war and turned into a country "primarily agricultural and pastoral in character". But this idea was vetoed by both the US state department and the British war cabinet.

Having failed with Roosevelt, Churchill flew to Moscow to meet Stalin himself, and on the back of an envelope agreed the proportion of their 'interest' in each liberated country. After the meeting an embarrassed Churchill urged Stalin to burn the envelope, afraid that it would look as if they had disposed of Europe's populations rather easily. "No, you keep it," joked Stalin.

Mortar fire across the Rhine at Strasbourg.

December 1944: American trucks destroyed during the Ardennes offensive.

ABOVE: **Stormtroopers searching US equipment, the Ardennes.** OPPOSITE: **Waving on the German advance.**

In particular, Churchill wanted to be able to guarantee the future of Greece, where 75,000 armed partisans were threatening to take control of the country. In a last-ditch attempt to stave off what he saw as Communism, Churchill braved a sniper-ridden Athens himself on Christmas Day and persuaded the resistance to accept the authority of Archbishop Damaskinos – whom he later described as a "scheming medieval prelate".

On the Western Front, the Allied delay had given Hitler a vital breathing space. He insisted on a counter-offensive in the Ardennes to break through Allied lines and force them back to the sea. "If Germany can deal a few heavy blows, this artificial coalition will collapse with a tremendous thunderclap," he assured his generals.

Allied decoding failed to pick up the coming onslaught. Montgomery had told his troops that the enemy "cannot stage major offensive operations", and Eisenhower was out playing golf. But on the morning of 16 December, with mist nullifying the Allied command of the air, groups of German commandos dressed in American uniform infiltrated the Allied

Montgomery and Eisenhower in a rare moment of accord.

replied "Nuts!" to a German request for surrender. Fearing that Bradley would not be able to control the forces to the north of the Germans, Eisenhower handed over command there to Montgomery, who infuriated the Americans by putting a large Union Jack on his car and riding to the 'rescue'. General Patton relieved Bastogne on Boxing Day 1944, while General de Gaulle, contradicting Eisenhower's order to retreat, held on to Strasbourg.

Hitler's Ardennes counter-offensive was defeated not only by obdurate Allied resistance, but by a fuel shortage: German tank crews were forced to abandon their vehicles and make their way back east on foot. Without fuel, Hitler could mount no more serious attempts to hold back the inevitable. Yet the war in Europe still had four months to run.

THE REICH IN ASHES

The Battle of Berlin and Hitler's Death

At Churchill's request, Stalin brought forward his offensive in the East by over a week to take the pressure off the Western Allies following the Battle of the Bulge. German intelligence had predicted a Russian push in the middle of January 1945, but Hitler refused to believe it. "It's the biggest imposture since Genghis Khan," he ranted. "Who is responsible for producing all this rubbish?" Guderian was left with just 50 infantry divisions to defend a 700-mile front.

In the falling snow, with as many as 200 divisions at their disposal, Zhukov and his fellow commanders surged forward 300 miles

into Germany. Resistance melted before them, and those German reinforcements that could be sent up the line were obstructed by fleeing civilians. But at the Oder river Stalin told Zhukov to halt and abandon the lightning thrust to Berlin he was planning. Meanwhile, Russian armies in the south finally took Budapest on 11 February – only to be pushed back from the Austrian border in March by the very last German offensive of the war.

As Soviet troops picked their way through the suburbs of the Hungarian capital, the three Allied leaders were putting the finishing touches to their agreement in Yalta. Churchill was again exasperated that his old friend Roosevelt (now a dying man) and potential

LEFT: **US troops crossing the Ruhr.**
OPPOSITE: **Exhausted German troops.**

ABOVE: February 1945 – US troops in newly-captured Julich. BELOW: Crossing the Rhine.

enemy Stalin managed such cordial relations. Stalin even agreed to the US plans for the United Nations. "We really believed in our hearts that this was the dawn of the new day we had all been praying for," said Roosevelt's adviser, Harry Hopkins.

British chiefs of staff, always pessimistic, were afraid the war might drag on until November: unity between the Allies had to be maintained. When they realized hostilities might end sooner, the British and Americans wished their leaders had bargained harder over the issue of Soviet-liberated territory. Churchill was particularly keen to see free elections in Poland – an idea that was completely unacceptable to Stalin.

Meanwhile, Sir Arthur Harris of Bomber Command had become impatient with the endless targeting of German fuel dumps and urged a return to the saturation bombing of German cities. It was to be his last chance to shatter civilian morale, and precipitated one of the darkest moments of the Allied war effort.

BELOW: Churchill arrives at the Rhine. ABOVE: Lunch by the river with Brooke and Montgomery.

ABOVE AND RIGHT: Russian troops on the outskirts of Budapest.

April 1945: the US Ninth Army meets the Red Army at Apollensdorf.

May 1945: Russians and Americans in Germany – a brief respite before the Cold War.

On 13 and 14 February, 1200 British and American bombers attacked the historic but strategically unimportant city of Dresden, then packed with refugees from the Russian front. The glow from the firestorms could be seen 200 miles away, and the city burned for a week. At least 40,000 people were killed, and possibly another 20,000 were incinerated beyond discovery. "How many died? Who knows the answer," reads the memorial in Dresden's cemetery. Even at the time, the results of the raid shocked Allied heads of staff, and unlike other senior officers, Arthur 'Bomber' Harris was never elevated to the peerage.

At sea, the Allied navies were still supporting operations in Italy and the south of France and continued to escort convoys to Russia via the Arctic and Black Sea. German U-boat strength reached its peak at this time, with 463 submarines operating in various parts of the globe.

At the beginning of March 1945, Finland, Egypt and Turkey all declared war on Germany. The odds the Nazis now faced served only to increase their fanaticism and cruelty. Executions of members of the Dutch resistance and civilian sympathizers were still taking place in those parts of Holland still under German control. And in desperation Hitler had started conscripting under-16s and was shifting the bulk of his forces from the Rhine to the Oder to meet the Russian 'barbarians'.

American troops march through the wreckage of a German town.

US troops in the outskirts of Koblenz.

Field Marshal von Rundstedt and his son in captivity at Augsburg.

Hungarian fascists surrender.

The way was clear for the western allies to cross the Rhine. On 7 March, Patton discovered a bridge intact across at Remagen. In a short time, a vital bridgehead was established on the other bank, which the Americans worked to expand in the following weeks. On 23 March, Montgomery's British and Canadian army in the north also crossed the river.

There was then a short pause in the Allied advance. Though Churchill urged Eisenhower to press ahead to Berlin before the Russians got there, the latter was more worried about rumours of a Nazi last stand in Bavaria (which never materialized). Elsewhere, the Germans fought a hard retreat, leaving their country devastated behind them. "The battle should be conducted without consideration for our own population," said Hitler.

On 12 April, Roosevelt died. Both Hitler and Goebbels believed they had been saved by a last-minute miracle ("God has not abandoned us," the propaganda minister is reported to have told the Fuhrer on the phone), but the Allied demands for unconditional surrender continued. The main German army was finally surrounded on the Ruhr, where 300,000 surrendered on 18 April following the suicide of the comman-

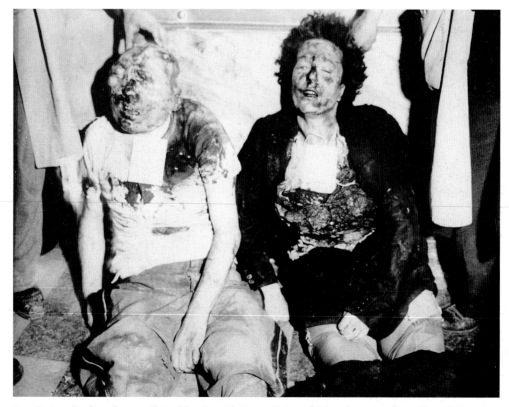

Partisans display the mutilated bodies of Mussolini and his mistress, Clara Petacci.

der-in-chief, Model. Having celebrated his birthday on 20 April, Hitler dismissed his remaining followers – furious that some were trying to negotiate a surrender (Himmler was even talking to the Red Cross, promising to send a number of Jews to Sweden in the hope of pleasing the Allies). Only Goebbels remained with Hitler in his Berlin bunker.

A week later, American and Soviet troops linked up at Torgau on the Elbe – a brief moment of camaraderie before the onset of the Cold War. Gun salutes were fired in Moscow, and there was

The Hindenburg Bridge in Cologne.

dancing and singing in New York's Times Square. But aware that Stalin's aim was to annex as much of Eastern Europe as possible before the surrender of Nazi Germany, the western Allies now accelerated their advance. "I deem it highly important that we should shake hands with the Russians as far to the east as possible," wrote Churchill to Eisenhower,

March 1945: American troops in Bonn.

ABOVE AND RIGHT: Russian troops enter Leipzig, eastern Germany.

The remains of Goering's house in the Berchtesgaden complex.

ordering Montgomery to press on to Hamburg and the Baltic while the French took Stuttgart and Patton raced towards Prague.

Stalin had already launched his own race to Berlin, urging Zhukov to attack from the east and Koniev from the south. Over two million Soviet troops pushed towards the German capital. Pale and puffy, Hitler sat hunched in bunker, his hands trembling, occasionally shouting meaningless orders and moving non-existent divisions around the map.

In Italy, German resistance was also beginning to collapse: Allied troops had finally crossed the Po. This success signalled a general uprising among Italian partisans, who proceeded to liberate Venice and Genoa. Meanwhile, Mussolini was trying to negotiate in Milan, carrying with him a large amount of money and letters with which he hoped to buy his freedom. Near Lake Como on the 28 April, he and his mistress Clara Petacci were taken from a German convoy by Italian partisans and shot. Their bodies were then mutilated and taken to Milan to be hung by the feet in the main square.

German forces in Italy finally surrendered on 29 April. Some 150,000 Italian partisans handed in their weapons to the Allies. The following day, American troops entered Munich, once the stronghold of Nazism, and were showered with white flowers. The radio station and other key installations had been seized by anti-Nazi Germans led by Captain Rupprecht Gerngross after a desperate struggle with the SS.

Realizing that the end was not far off, the same day Hitler ordered Goering's arrest for trying to negotiate with the Allies and appointed Doenitz as his successor. Then he married Eva Braun and wrote his will. "I charge the leaders of the nation and those under them to scrupulous observance of the laws of the race," he wrote, "and to merciless opposition to the universal poisoner of all peoples, International Jewry."

Soviet T-34 tanks and ISU-152 self-propelled guns in the streets of East Berlin.

At 3.30pm the following day, 30 April, Hitler said goodbye to the bunker staff and shut himself in his room. He then shot himself; Eva Braun took poison. What happened next is still unclear. In the German account, the bodies were doused with petrol and cremated. The Russians, on the other hand, claimed they captured the corpses and photographed them, destroying them only later. Either way, no remains have ever come to light.

Even a German PoW is delighted by the news.

Across the city, Goebbels followed Hitler's example and gave his entire family poison before killing himself. After a last stand at the Berlin zoo, the remaining German forces in the city surrendered. Doenitz tried to negotiate a surrender in the West while fighting on in the East, but Eisenhower vetoed the idea. On 4 May, the German armies of the north surrendered to Montgomery on Luneburg Heath. Three days later, General Jodl was in Reims to sign Eisenhower's unconditional

ABOVE: Kinzel signing the surrender of the northern armies at Luneburg Heath.
LEFT: The hammer and sickle is raised on the Reichstag.

A German civilian reads the announcement of VE Day. Opposite: **Churchill celebrates in London.**

surrender of all German forces. On VE Day, 8 May, there was immense public rejoicing in both Times Square and Trafalgar Square.

But the fighting in Europe was not quite over. In Prague, the Czechs had risen against the Nazi occupiers but, since the new US President Harry Truman refused to risk American lives for 'political' purposes, Patton was ordered to halt on the outskirts of the city. By a strange twist of fate, Prague was liberated from the SS by General Vlasov and his Russian Liberation Army, which had been fighting alongside the Germans for most of the war. It failed to secure Vlasov and his followers their hoped-for reprieve: they were executed when Soviet troops arrived on 12 May.

More fighting seemed about to break out around Trieste, when both Churchill and Truman were prepared to use force to keep the city out of Tito's hands. But without Stalin's support, Tito decided not to hold on and his partisans left on 9 June. The two great armies of the Communist and democratic powers now faced each other across the rubble and wreckage of liberated Europe.

HOLOCAUST

The Discovery of the Death Camps

At the beginning of April 1945, troops of an American armoured division outside Gotha encountered what they described as "cadaverous refugees" on the road. These Jewish 'refugees', shaven-headed and skeletal, guided the Americans to Ohrdruf where there were piles of corpses in striped uniforms. Each victim had been shot in the back of the head by fleeing Nazi guards. General Eisenhower visited the camp shortly afterwards and was so shocked that he phoned Churchill to describe the appalling scene.

Anyone with the least interest in current events had been aware of the Nazi persecution of Jews from the very beginning of Hitler's rule. Newspapers over the world had reported how the Jewish middle class – intellectuals, financiers, physicians – had been forced out of public life.

Poland – prisoners transported in cattle trucks.

Camp inmates after liberation.

US troops hand out cigarettes at one of the camps.

They knew that Nazis regarded Arabs, Africans, Slavs and Orientals in general as *untermenschen* (subhuman), but that they reserved their special venom for Jews. "The Jew's features resemble man," wrote one Nazi theorist, "but intellectually, spiritually, he is lower than an animal."

Hitler had deprived Jews of German citizenship and basic human rights as far back as 1935. They were forbidden to go to concerts or films, to drive, to sit on park benches or buy newspapers; marrying an 'Aryan' was punishable by death. Hatred of Jewry culminated in the infamous *Krystallnacht* ('night of broken glass') of 1938, which took place after a Jewish youth assassinated the German ambassador to Paris. Thousands of synagogues and Jewish businesses were looted and burned while the police looked on.

Concentration camps such as Dachau had been set up as early as 1933, though as yet there was no policy of genocide. Socialists, Jehovah's

Conditions inside a camp barracks.

Witnesses, homosexuals, gypsies and pacifists all joined the Jews behind barbed wire. But with Hitler's conquests of 1939-41, the number of Jews under German rule increased to up to 10 million. Hitler planned to resettle them in Madagascar, though by this stage tens of thousands had

The terrible evidence: bodies in an extermination camp.

The remains of the camp sidings at Nordhausen.

A concentration camp commandant is taken prisoner.

Jewish child survivors leave Buchenwald for France – then on to Palestine.

On their way home: Rumanian survivors of Buchenwald in Vienna.

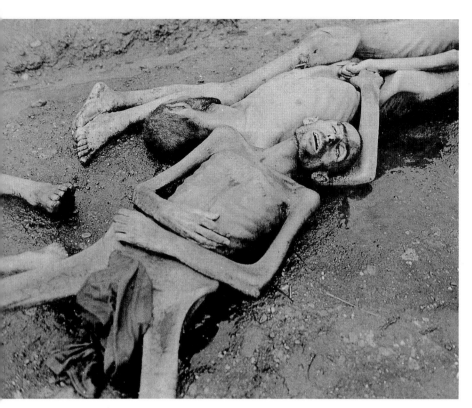

ABOVE: **The camera was one witness that did not flinch.**

already been murdered in Poland and Russia. "By exterminating this pest, we shall do humanity a service of which our soldiers can have no idea," the Führer remarked.

It was not until 1942 that Himmler unveiled what he described as the 'Final Solution' – the extermination of the Jewish race in Europe. Death camps would be set up which would utilize industrial techniques to 'process' Jews. The names of these camps would later be branded on human consciousness as bywords for unspeakable inhumanity: Dachau, Treblinka, Auschwitz, Belsen and many others.

Victims were rounded up, told they were being resettled and ordered to bring food for three days' travel. They were then herded into cattle trucks with almost no water. Tens of thousands died long before they reached the camps.

On arrival at their destination, the survivors were divided between the healthy and infirm. The healthy were used as slave labour. Life expectancy for these inmates was no more than three to six months before they died from exhaustion, starvation or the brutality of well-fed SS guards. On the other hand, most of the 'weak' – women, children and old people – were promptly forced to undress and marched into a 'shower room'. Then Zyklon-B poison gas, developed by a large German pharmaceutical company, was pumped in above them. The victims' bodies, blue-faced with suffocation, were processed by other inmates. Gold teeth were pulled, hair was shorn for mattress stuffing, and clothing was sent back to Germany for distribution. Bones were crushed for fertilizer and

The dead and the soon-to-die.

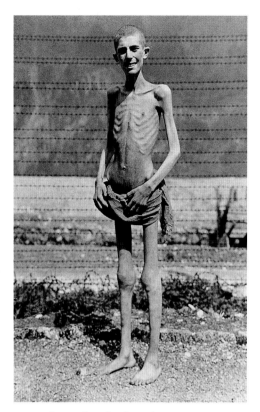

A survivor – but for how long?

human fat was melted down for soap.

The reality of the Holocaust was known in part to the Allies, and in December 1942 a joint statement by Britain, the USA, the Soviet Union and General de Gaulle's French National Committee condemned "this bestial policy of cold-blooded extermination". Leaflets outlining the atrocities were dropped over Berlin in 1943.

As the war began to go against them, the Nazis began to worry about Allied retribution. "The whole operation must be speeded up, considerably speeded up," fretted Hitler as early as August 1942, when he was shown round an extermination camp. But by the following summer, Himmler had enough doubts about the future to order the systematic destruction of evidence of mass murder. Slave labourers were forced to revisit the sites of executions, dig the corpses up and incinerate them having first extracted their gold teeth.

The Jewish reaction to this hell was at first bewilderment. Even as they were transported, many refused to believe that they faced any fate worse than hard labour (the death camps were often disguised as work camps). The terrible truth began to sink in only slowly. "Who has inflicted this upon us? Who has made us Jews different to all other people? Who has allowed us to suffer so terribly up to now?" wrote the 14 year-old Anne Frank in her diary, as she hid with her parents and her sister in Amsterdam in 1944. She died in Belsen the following year.

In the summer of 1944, four inmates from Auschwitz managed to escape and smuggle details of the camp to neutral Switzerland. The reports were read with horror by Churchill and his foreign secretary Anthony Eden, but their requests to bomb the railway lines were rejected as too risky by the RAF and the US Airforce. The Americans did drop leaflets on Budapest warning the Hungarians that anyone responsible for persecuting the Jews would be punished and, within two days, Admiral Horthy had stopped the deportations. Yet by then, 437,000 Hungarian Jews had already been sent north.

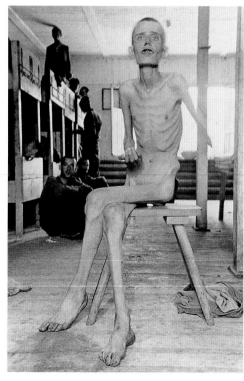

Living skeletons.

US troops face the truth.

When the Americans entered Buchenwald on 11 April 1945, finding that the guards had fled, they found thousands of starving survivors. Four days later, the British entered Belsen. They found 35,000 sticklike corpses and 30,000 emaciated survivors; in the following weeks, 300 a day died of starvation and typhoid. On 28 April, the Americans arrived at Dachau. All 500 Nazi guards were killed shortly afterwards, some by the inmates and some by US troops appalled by the 50 railway wagons they found filled with bodies beside the crematorium.

The fate of six million European Jews, as well as hundreds of thousands of gypsies, homosexuals and political dissidents, constitutes one of the great horror stories of history. But the Holocaust could not have taken place without the active involvement of police, bureaucrats and civilians in a number of occupied countries. Afraid of reprisals against Roman Catholics, the Pope also failed to intervene.

There were some German heroes, such as Anton Schid and Oscar Schindler; and not every one in the Reich participated through silence in the Jews' fate. "There have been some regrettable scenes at a home for

Bare subsistence in the ruins of the camps.

Local Germans forced to confront the mass graves.

Exhuming bodies in the lime-pits.

aged Jews," wrote Goebbels in his diary in 1943, "when a large number of people gathered and some of them even sided with the Jews." Indeed, there were large acts of rebellion on the Jews' behalf. The people of Amsterdam held a general strike to support them as early as 1941. After pressure from Finnish religious leaders and politicians in early 1943, the Finnish cabinet – though their troops were fighting with the Germans in Russia – refused any more deportations. In September 1943, nearly all of Denmark's Jewish population was smuggled by fisherman over the water to Sweden. (One of these was the nuclear scientist Niels Bohr, who would later play a leading role in the development of the atomic bomb.) And among the many who hid Jews in their homes in Greece was Prince Philip's mother, Princess Andrew.

Despite the vast scale of the military conflict, the Holocaust must overshadow any history of World War II. The enormity of this systematic genocide, and the horrible logic with which it was pursued, continues to beggar both description and analysis. The camps' discoverers were rendered all but speechless. "I pray you believe what I have seen," said the American broadcaster Ed Murrow, speaking on radio from Buchenwald. "I reported what I saw and you heard only part of it. For most of it, I have no words."

Inmates celebrate following liberation.

THE PACIFIC
THE RISE AND FALL OF THE JAPANESE EMPIRE

JAPANESE EXPANSIONISM
The War in China

The Japanese now know the period of militarism and war which ended with their defeat in 1945 as *kurai tanima*, or the 'dark valley'. But the roots of the Pacific War have their beginnings in a dark valley shared by most of the world. On 29 October 1929, the value of shares collapsed on Wall Street in New York, and a two and a half year economic slide began that would have global repercussions and come to be known as the Great Depression.

In 1932, facing the worst economic collapse in history, the British announced a range of protective tariffs and extended these to their colonies; the following year, the newly-elected US president, Franklin Roosevelt, devalued the dollar and began a desperate bid for recovery, unconcerned about the effect it might have on other countries. Nations

Japanese troops in training.

'Making an example': Japanese troops bayonet Chinese PoWs.

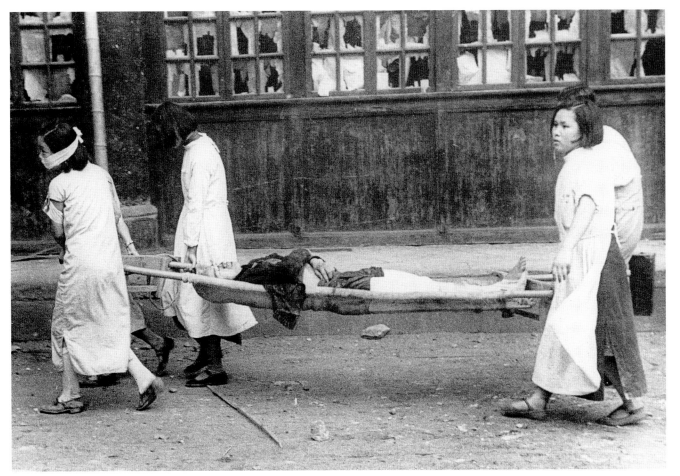

Chinese stretcher-bearers after a Japanese raid.

Japanese troops arrive in Tsinan.

Chungking after Japanese bombing.

ABOVE: August 1937 – air raids on Shanghai. BELOW: Japanese marines in the streets of Shanghai.

LEFT AND ABOVE: Street-fighting in Shanghai.

ABOVE: Japanese troops push through the Shanghai rubble. BELOW: A Japanese armoured car.

Japanese troops scrambling over the twisted remains of the Tientsin-Pukow railway.

The Japanese destroyer *Tsuta* on the Hai-Ho River.

alliance. The Japanese quickly occupied the cities of Peking and Tientsin and, in August their troops landed outside the vital port of Shanghai. In the attack which followed, the American gunboat *Panay* was sunk and the British ambassador injured. In an attempt to cut the country in two, the Japanese pushed on up the Yangtze River. On 13 December, they had taken Chiang's own capital city, Nanking. An orgy of slaughter followed.

In northern China, a Japanese advance from Manchuria was halted by an unexpected counter-attack by Chiang at Taierchwang, in the course of which 20,000 Japanese were killed. It was modern Japan's

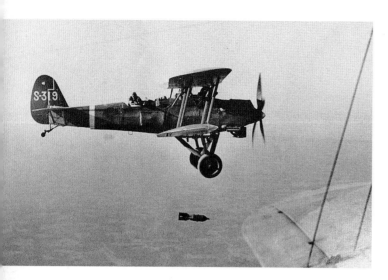

ABOVE: A Japanese bomber and its effect.
OPPOSITE: Chinese refugees escape the bombing.

first major military defeat. The advance continued, however, and Chinese commanders were forced to break the dikes on the Yellow River near Chengchow, flooding the whole region and drowning tens of thousands. The Japanese advance became bogged down in a sea of mud.

Eventually, the Japanese took the strategically vital cities of Suchow in the north and Hanchow in the south – effectively squeezing China in an enormous vice. In October 1938 they took Canton, which had replaced Shanghai as China's most important trade outlet. By the end of the year, the Japanese controlled the whole Chinese coastline, and Chiang had withdrawn to the Tibetan border.

During this first phase of the Sino-Japanese war, the sufferings of civilians were atrocious. Casualty figures are unreliable, but some claims put the number of Chinese people killed at 800,000, with up to 50 million (about 10 per cent of the total population) driven from their homes.

Newsreel audiences around the world were appalled by the images of carnage and cruelty. International diplomats could reach no kind of settlement to stop the fighting: the main stumbling-block appeared to be that Japan had not actually declared war. Moreover, the West simply did not want to become actively involved in the conflict.

The Chinese and Japanese armies now changed their strategy: the former settled down to a guerilla war of attrition, destroying Japanese supply lines wherever possible, while the latter resolved on a policy of slow strangulation – blockading ports and closing the land-routes into China.

In the summer of 1938, the Japanese also launched two offensives against the Russians in Manchuria: both were knocked back with heavy losses. Japanese army strategists realized that, if the flag of the Rising Sun was going to be hoisted anywhere else, it would have to be to the east of their country – in the Pacific.

THE RISING SUN

JAPANESE VICTORIES
IN THE PACIFIC

'DAY OF INFAMY'

The Japanese Strike at Pearl Harbor

"The rise and fall of the empire depends upon this battle," signalled Yamamoto to his attack fleet before the strike at Pearl Harbor. But even at this stage, not everything was going to plan. Attack fleet commander Admiral Chuichi Nagumo had just been informed that the American aircraft carriers were not at their moorings, as intelligence had indicated, but were elsewhere in the Pacific on a training exercise. Nonetheless, he decided the attack should go ahead. There were also to be attacks on the US Pacific island bases on Guam, Wake and Midway, and on the British strongholds of Singapore and Hong Kong.

Shortly after dawn on 7 December 1941, 423 Japanese aircraft took off

Warming up on the flight deck of the *Kiryu* before the attack.

318

An aerial view of Pearl Harbor prior to the Japanese attack.

from the decks of the six aircraft carriers of the Japanese fleet. By 7.55 am, they were over Pearl Harbor. Below them lay the American Pacific Fleet, including eight US battleships unprotected by torpedo nets, anchored in neat rows – the regulation practice in peacetime. Each Japanese pilot carried with him a cheap picture postcard of the base, divided into squares to show his specific target area.

The Americans had little or no warning: Pearl Harbor's radar had

Nagumo: the attack commander.

A Japanese Kate torpedo bomber over Pearl Harbor.

shut down for church parade and the anti-aircraft ammunition was locked away. The attack came in two great waves, the dive-bombers and torpedo planes wreaking havoc on their sitting targets. Two hours later, four American battleships lay on the harbour bottom, and four more had been seriously damaged; 188 US planes had been destroyed or put out of action on the ground; and over 3500 American servicemen had been killed or injured. Hanging over the base was a huge pall of oily smoke that could be seen from miles out to sea.

Zeros massed on deck of a Japanese carrier.

ABOVE AND BELOW: The attack in progress.

Wrecked battleships of the US Pacific Fleet.

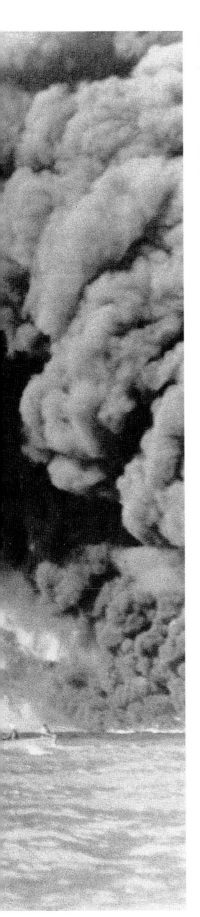

Flak over Pearl Harbor during the attack.

The sky is clear of raiders, but the base continues to burn.

Such was the degree of surprise achieved that only 29 attacking planes were shot down. "Leaving aside the unspeakable treachery of it, the Japanese did a fine job," judged fleet commander Admiral Husband Kimmel, later relieved of his command. Up to 18 days after the attack, sailors were still being cut out alive from the capsized hull of the battleship *West Virginia*.

By one of the strange ironies of war, the Japanese government had planned to actually declare war on the USA half an hour before the air strike began, and diplomats in the Japanese embassy in Washington had been slaving away over the translation. But they missed the deadline, and a shamefaced Japanese ambassador was forced to deliver the declaration while the attack was in progress.

Stricken battleships: *West Virginia*, *Tennessee* and *Arizona*.

ABOVE AND BELOW: The remains of two US battleships.

OPPOSITE: Pearl Harbor air base after the attack.

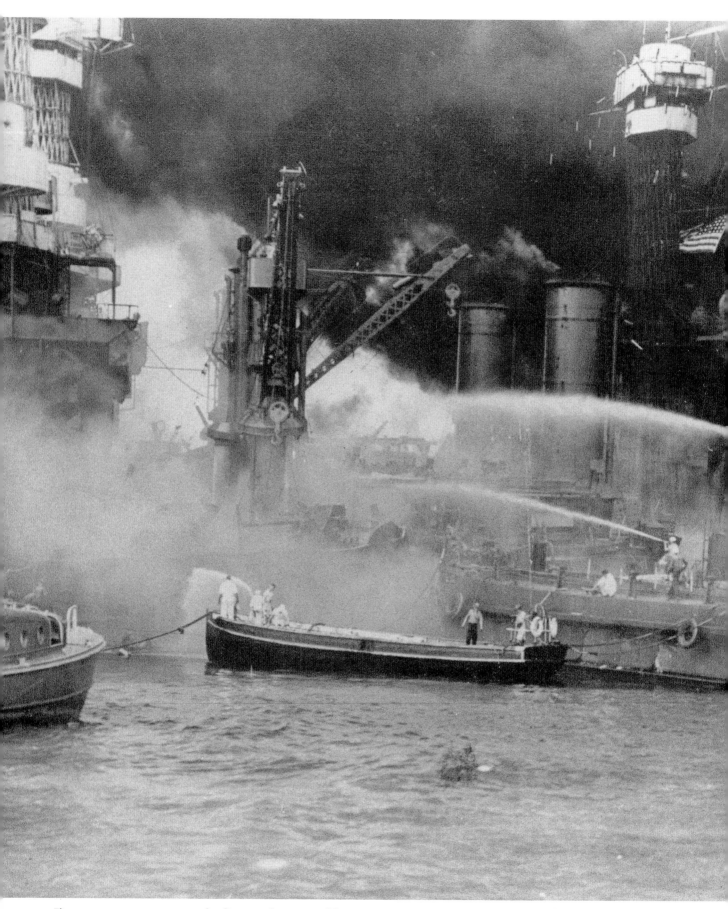

Firemen attempt to put out the fires on the USS *California*.

US sailors look on helplessly as a neighbouring battleship burns.

Warnings from US Navy commanders on duty in the Pacific, who had sensed from intercepted signals that a Japanese attack was due at dawn somewhere, had been sent to Washington. But a series of bizarre accidents and misunderstandings meant that these warnings were not passed on to Pearl Harbor in time (the crucial message was sent by commercial cable, and was arriving by motorbike messenger just as the first bombs and torpedoes were falling). Some of these muddles were so peculiar that historians have claimed that President Roosevelt deliberately delayed the warnings in order to bring America into the war. But this seems highly improbable: incompetence and complacency seem the more likely villains.

The day after the attack, the president addressed the nation.

Carnage at Pearl Harbor air base, Hickam Field.

The remains of a US seaplane.

ABOVE: Rueful US anti-aircraft gunners among the wreckage of Hickam Field. OPPOSITE: The *Missouri*.

Number 11 hanger at Hickam Field.

"Yesterday, December 7 – a day which will live in infamy – the United States was suddenly and deliberately attacked by naval and air forces of the Empire of Japan," he said, his voice shaking with anger. "No matter how long it may take us to overcome this premeditated invasion, the American people in their righteous might will win through to absolute victory." In Tokyo on the day of the attack, Tojo had broadcast to the Japanese people using similar phraseology. "I promise you final victory," he said.

Meanwhile in Berlin, the brutality of the Japanese air strike thrilled

Scanning the skies for another attack.

The remains of a Flying Fortress.

A civilian car in Hawaii strafed by Japanese fighters.

Burying US Navy personnel.

The *Prince of Wales* under attack.

air power had changed naval warfare; it also meant there was now no significant Allied naval force in the Pacific theatre to oppose the Japanese. "In all the war, I never received a more direct shock," wrote Churchill later. "Over all this vast expanse of waters, Japan was supreme and we everywhere were weak and naked."

British colonial centres, meanwhile, were facing bombardment from the air (over 600 civilians were killed in a Japanese raid on Penang in Malaya on 12 December) and the defenders of Hong Kong now knew the Japanese troops were as close as Kowloon. Although British strategists had realized Hong Kong was probably indefensible, they had still sent two Canadian battalions in a desperate last-ditch attempt to defend it. Even as they arrived, the hard-pressed Hong Kong governor Sir Mark Young was turning down Japanese demands for unconditional surrender.

Japanese troops and engineers advance towards Singapore.

Japanese troops rush into Hong Kong.

On 18 December, the Japanese landed on Hong Kong island. When the colony finally surrendered on Christmas Day 1941, 11,000 prisoners were taken, and westerners witnessed at first hand the brutality of the emperor's soldiery. Prisoners were roped together *en masse* and bayoneted to death; the victims included hospital staff and 'looters'. The fate of the colony sent shock waves through in the region. For the first time, the true extent and nature of Japanese ambitions were becoming clear.

"We refuse to accept that the Pacific struggle must be treated as a subordinate segment of the general conflict," wrote furious Australian Prime Minister, John Curtin, to Allied heads of staff on 27 December, as he contemplated the comparative defencelessness of his country. But the loss of the *Prince of Wales* and *Repulse* had also seriously weakened the defensive capabilities of Singapore. A new command known as ABDA – American, British, Dutch, Australian – was hastily put together to resist the Japanese onslaught in South-East Asia, though the forces at their disposal were worryingly small. At sea, there was only a small fleet of cruisers, destroyers and submarines to cover a vast area, and they had no common signals or techniques. But during January 1942, ABDA ships escort-

Japanese commanders parade through the streets of Hong Kong.

Yamashita: the conqueror of Malaya.

ed 45,000 troops to Malaya, while the British aircraft carrier *Indomitable* ferried Hurricane aircraft to reinforce Java.

In command of the Japanese assault on Malaya was General Tomoyuki Yamashita, who had spent the previous Christmas in Germany studying Hitler's *Blitzkrieg* tactics. But the use of heavy armour was inappropriate to the often thickly forested terrain of the Far East. Yamashita made a typically resourceful (and cheap) adaptation: he armed his troops with bicycles. These allowed fast movement along the narrow jungle tracks, and could be carried if necessary in the more impassable sectors. By advancing directly through the jungle instead of along the heavily defended roads, his troops sought to take the British and Commonwealth troops by surprise.

Sure enough, Yamashita's tactics worked and the Japanese advance down the west coast of Malaya was rapid. As the British general Sir Archibald Wavell arrived from Africa to take command of the ABDA forces in the whole region, 40,000 British and Indian troops found themselves cut off and captured in central Malaya. On 31

ABOVE AND OPPOSITE: *Blitzkrieg* by bicycle – Japanese troops in Malaya.

January, the British commander in Malaya, Arthur Percival, withdrew all troops to Singapore island, and awaited the Japanese attack.

The conquest of Malaya had taken Yamashita just 54 days, and cost him just 4600 troops. Painful as the loss of the colony was, Churchill refused to believe that Singapore itself could fall and continued to send reinforcements. Then, on the night of 8 February, the first Japanese troops on inflatable rafts made it across across the channel dividing Singapore from the mainland (others swam across with their equipment

Disarming a British soldier in the forest.

on their backs) and the defenders were taken by surprise. By dawn on the 9 February, 13,000 Japanese had landed, while the Japanese air force pounded the city. The British commanders were suddenly the target of a series of appeals from London that the "battle should be fought to the bitter end at all costs".

"Our whole fighting reputation is at stake and the honour of the British Empire," said Wavell in a message to the defenders. But during an air raid he injured his back falling downstairs and had to be shipped out. Percival was left to make the promise to Churchill "to fight to the last man"; but a week later, with food and water supplies running low, he had to face the fact that, unless a complete massacre was to take place, surrender was inevitable.

He went in person to Yamashita under a white flag, believing that he could guarantee humane treatment for the people of Singapore. This was a forlorn hope: Japanese troops promptly rounded up and murdered 5000 prominent Chinese civilians. As for Percival's own troops (32,000 Indians, 16,000 British and 14,000 Australians), though their lives were spared, their treatment was atrocious: by the end of the war, more than

LEFT: Parading through the streets of Singapore. ABOVE: Yamashita accepts the surrender.

ABOVE AND BELOW: Indian and British PoWs after the collapse of resistance in Singapore.

half had died in the infamous Changi jail or been worked to death in the sun.

The loss of Singapore was not only a bitter blow to British military pride, it exposed the fragility of the Empire. All Churchill could do was urge the British people to "display the calm and poise, combined with grim determination, which not so long ago brought us out of the very jaws of death". In Japan, on the other hand, the victory was greeted with mass jubilation; by a special order, every home in the country had to fly the flag of the Rising Sun. But Tojo became jealous of the adulation received by Yamashita, and any mention of his name was later for-

PoWs facing a grim internment.

bidden by the military administration. Yamashita himself was 'exiled' to the relatively inactive border between Japanese Manchuria and Russia, where he remained until 1944.

British PoWs forced to wait in the sun after the surrender.

STRIKING SOUTH

Japanese Gains in South-East Asia

In the enforced lull between Pearl Harbor and the opportunity to hit back at the enemy across the Pacific, the American people soon became frustrated. Immediate revenge was required. The only perceived 'enemy' within reach were of course the Japanese-Americans. In draconian measures rushed through Congress, all Japanese-American families were given 48 hours to sell their homes and businesses and move to distant detention camps, where they were to remain until the end of the

On American submarine patrol.

ABOVE: The powerful new Japanese battleship *Yamato*. BELOW: Naval minister Shimada.

war. Such racist hysteria was perhaps understandable given the shock of Pearl Harbor, but it was also plainly wrong (the US government later apologized and paid compensation to all families).

For the time being, the American administration was more intent on boosting war production. In the first six months of 1942, Roosevelt's government, urged on by Churchill and Lord Beaverbrook, placed orders totalling more than $100 billion in war equipment – more than the entire US GNP. Donald Nelson, the purchasing vice-president of Sears Roebuck, was appointed to lead the War Production Board and given unprecedented powers.

Even so, it was clear that the resources to make war across the vast expanses of the Pacific would not be ready for some time. The US Pacific Fleet had to be reconstituted – and it would face a Japanese navy which even before the war had been the third most powerful in the world. Thanks to Admiral Yamamoto, the

American civilians on Wake Island go into captivity.

Japanese naval parachutists in the Dutch East Indies.

Japanese troops dash ashore in North Borneo.

The Dutch colonial army.

Japanese also had one of the most modern carrier fleets and the best-trained naval pilots. As late as mid-1941, they had been busily developing three of the world's most powerful battleships, each equipped with enormous 18.1 inch guns. The first of the trio, *Yamato*, was due for completion in early 1942.

But Yamamoto's navy also had a series of disadvantages. For one thing, it had still not developed a workable naval radar – a lack that would later prove extremely costly. It was also going to be heavily dependent on its merchant fleet to transport oil from its envisaged conquests. These ships would be highly vulnerable to US submarine attack – though Japanese naval planners nursed the fantasy that American servicemen were too 'soft' to endure the rigours of submarine warfare. Thirdly, there was little confidence in Japan's own fleet of submarines, following their failure to score any hits in the attack on Pearl Harbor. And last but not least, the Japanese navy had suffered an early setback: at Wake Atoll, the invasion force escorts had accidentally come within range of the shore batteries of the US Marines, and three destroyers were lost.

A Japanese parade in Kendai in the Celebes.

Putting up the new notices in Japanese.

In January 1942, the US Navy carried out its first offensive action of the Pacific War, when the carrier *Enterprise* struck at Japanese bases on the Marshall Islands. But the *Enterprise* was damaged in the process, and the Americans withdrew to consider future strategy.

The expected Japanese attack on the oil-rich Dutch East Indies came soon afterwards, on 10 January, when forces under General Imamura landed at Tarakan in Borneo and Manado in the Celebes, their convoys harried by Dutch planes and submarines. On 9 February, a Japanese convoy aimed at Sumatra set sail from Indo-China, and in pursuit of it ABDA's naval forces fought a series of disastrous actions now known collectively as the Battle of the Java Sea.

Co-ordinating the ships of four nations was difficult enough, but the

A Japanese soldier watches burning oil tanks in Tanjong, Java.

February 1942: wounded Dutch servicemen are brought ashore in Java.

Japanese infantry dash past the wreckage of a British plane.

Japanese troops are cheered by local Burmese as they enter Tavoy.

Japanese bicycle troops cross the Panga River.

Dutch admiral in command of the force, Karel Doorman, had almost no air cover and had reckoned without the effectiveness of the new Japanese 'long lance' torpedoes. The force was attacked by Japanese planes on 4 February and, such was the damage sustained, had to withdraw. So Doorman found himself 800 miles away from Sumatra when the Japanese invasion began on 14 February. Then, on 26 and 27 February, he fought a series of engagements with the escorts for the Japanese invasion force bound for Java. Doorman himself was drowned when his flagship *De Ruyter* went down; the stragglers fell victim to Japanese

March 1942: Japanese troops arrive on Christmas Island.

bombers and by 1 March, the whole force had been wiped out. The Japanese now had total control of the sea.

Dutch Borneo, New Guinea and the Celebes were the next European colonies to fall. Once again, relatively small detachments of Japanese troops were able to overwhelm the defenders; once again captured Dutch, British and Australian troops were shot or bayoneted to death. Within seven weeks the Japanese had also captured Macassar, Timor, Sumatra and Java. In Java, 25,000 Dutch troops had faced not only the invading Japanese but serious civil disobedience from nationalists as they awaited the Japanese 'liberators'. By 8 March 1942, the ABDA command had been wound up in the Dutch East Indies and some 100,000 Dutch, British and Australian troops had been taken prisoner (nearly a quarter were to die in captivity).

LEFT AND ABOVE: Japanese invaders arrive in the British colony of Burma.

The Japanese were now the rulers of some 100 million people in South-East Asia, and their command of the sea extended from the Australian coast (Darwin had been bombarded on 19 February) to the Bay of Bengal. Near Ceylon they threatened the British Eastern Fleet consisting of five ancient battleships and three aircraft carriers. Its new commander, Admiral Sir James Somerville, had tried to put a good face on the fact that his ships were hopelessly outmoded. "There's many a good tune played on an old fiddle," he said.

But Somerville did have access to Japanese naval codes, and so he was warned that a powerful carrier fleet was out to find him; he was thus able

Japanese troops survey the remains of a British tank, Burma.

A Japanese 'trial' of villagers in the Burmese jungle.

The Japanese using local labour to aid their advance.

to take his own to a secret anchorage 600 miles south-west of Ceylon at Addu Atoll, and avoid the Japanese air attack on Colombo on Easter Day 1942. But soon afterwards, the Royal Navy received another lesson in the vulnerability of ships to air attack. Japanese planes sighted one of his carriers, *Hermes*, in the Bay of Bengal, and sank it with 40 bombs in just 10 minutes. Two Royal Navy cruisers were also destroyed, including the *Dorsetshire*, which had administered the *coup de grâce* to the German battleship *Bismarck* the previous year.

Far to the north, other catastrophes had been taking place in Burma, where 35,000 Japanese troops had arrived at the end of 1941. Burma was vital to the continued resistance of the Chinese (the Burma Road was their main supply route) but as the Japanese approached, disorder began to spread in this now disaffected British colony. The Rangoon police began to desert, armed thugs emerged and declared their backing for the Japanese, and when the air raids began the civil administration went to pieces. Worse still, the British

TOP AND ABOVE: Admiral Somerville and the last moments of HMS *Hermes*.

Japanese close in on the Burma oil fields.

had only 16 aircraft to go up against the Japanese air attacks and the urgently created Burma Observer Corps had no radio sets, and were forced to report using the inefficient public phone network. Wavell, who was also commander-in-chief in India, also offended Chiang Kai-shek when he turned down the offer of two Chinese defence armies on the grounds that they came without transport or supplies.

Completely new to jungle warfare, the British fought alongside Indian troops and Gurkhas in the north of the country until they found them-

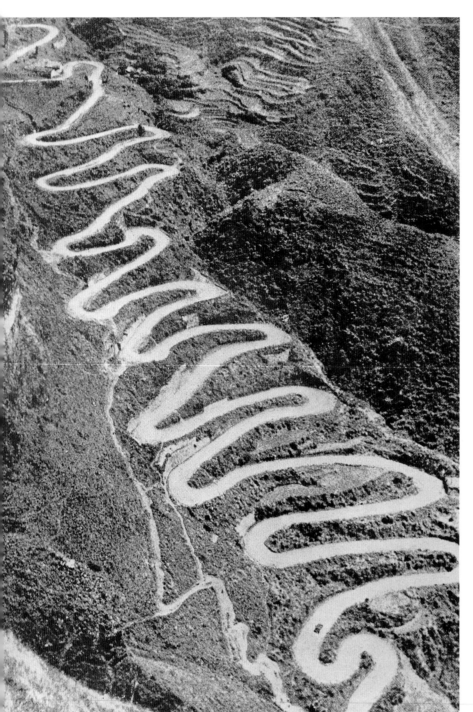

Chiang Kai-shek's supply route: the Burma Road.

selves forced to retreat over the Sittang River, blowing the bridge as they went. Their commanders, meanwhile, agonized over whether to make a stand at Rangoon or Mandalay. At this point, the new supreme commander, Sir Harold Alexander, arrived and decided (having himself escaped by the skin of his teeth from his headquarters in Rangoon) that the defence of India was the priority: Burma might have to be abandoned completely. When Japanese troops finally entered Rangoon on 8 March, they found it empty of British troops.

ABOVE: The Japanese crossing Burmese rivers in the course of their advance.

Alexander reversed Wavell's policy towards Chiang, but when the American general Stilwell arrived in Burma at the head of the promised Chinese armies, all he could do was delay the Japanese advance until the monsoon in May – which all westerners had hoped would halt operations in the region. On 29 April, both Alexander and Stilwell were appalled to hear that the Japanese had cut the Burma Road at Lashio. There was now no way back to China.

British, Indian and Chinese troops then began a series of gruelling

ABOVE AND BELOW: Japanese troops cross the Chindwin River during the monsoon.

ABOVE: Allied troops retreating down the Chindwin. BELOW: General Slim.

retreats by foot east through the Burmese hills to the Indian border. On 11 May, 60,000 troops of General William Slim's Burma Corps crossed the Chindwin River to make the 1000-mile march through the hills to Assam, their boots giving out and their uniforms in rags. Stilwell's 100,000 Chinese followed, passing the decaying bodies of refugees along the way. Stilwell and his staff arrived two weeks later, having made the last 150 miles on foot through the slippery mountain passes. They were met with bald indifference by the British authorities in India. "They were utterly exhausted, riddled with malaria and dysentery," wrote Slim, "and deserved something better than the complete lack of consideration or help which they received." Stilwell agreed: "We got a hell of a beating. We got run out of Burma and it is humiliating. We ought to find out why it happened, go back and retake it."

DEFEAT IN THE PHILIPPINES

The Surrender of the US Army

America's most senior general, Douglas MacArthur – wearing a uniform he had designed himself and with his hair dyed black – had been sent to take command of the vital US bases in the Philippines in the summer of 1941. A Japanese attack had always been expected there, but once war was underway MacArthur's defences were soon undermined. Hours after the air strike at Pearl Harbor, the US Far Eastern Air Force was attacked at its bases in the Philippines and largely destroyed on the ground. At one stroke, the Japanese had command of the skies over the islands. On 10 December 1941, the first of 57,000 Japanese troops under General Masaharu Homma started landing on the tip of the island of Luzon.

December 1941: Homma arrives in the Philippines.

May 1942: American and Filipino PoWs at Corregidor.

Homma's army was less than half the size of the MacArthur's, but his troops were highly trained and better equipped. MacArthur had also concentrated his regulars outside Manila, which meant Homma had little trouble overcoming the Filipino soldiers dispersed around the coastline watching for the invasion.

On Christmas Eve 1941, persistent air bombardment forced MacArthur to retreat from Manila and declare it an open city; Japanese troops walked into it on 2 January 1942.

MacArthur resolved to dig in on the Bataan peninsula, a swampy tract

LEFT AND ABOVE: Damage to the US naval base of Cavite on Luzon.

Spent American AA shells on Cavite.

Japanese troops charge US positions at Subic Bay, outside Manila.

of land 25 miles long by 20 miles wide and dominated by the fortified island of Corregidor. He set up his headquarters on the island, together with the Filipino president, Manuel Quezon. Meanwhile, US troops in Bataan received their first taste of tropical warfare, battling not just the Japanese but diseases such as hookworm, beri-beri, dysentery and malaria. "Help is on its way from the United States," MacArthur comforted the worn-out defenders. "Thousands of troops and hundreds of planes are being despatched."

But the general was wrong. The Japanese now controlled the Pacific sea-lanes and, besides, strategic planners in Washington had judged that the Philippines could no longer be defended. Any further troops or

The Cavite naval base, abandoned in the face of the Japanese attack.

MacArthur and President Quezon in Bataan.

Refugees leave a burning Manila.

Top AND ABOVE: **Japanese troops on the outskirts of Manila.**

ABOVE AND BELOW: Japanese forces on the march outside Manila.

equipment sent there would simply fall into the hands of the Japanese.

MacArthur's position worsened. His original plans provided for 43,000 defenders, but he found the narrow strip of Bataan now contained as many as 100,000 troops and refugees. Disease also meant that only a quarter of his army were well enough to fight. On the other side, Homma had a similar problem, with 10,000 troops sick and one division removed from his command and sent to the Dutch East Indies. There was a brief cessation of hostilities.

On 11 March 1942, Roosevelt ordered MacArthur to leave Corregidor. "I shall return," he vowed, once he had escaped by torpedo boat to Australia. The defenders, now the self-styled 'Battling Bastards of

The streets of Manila following Japanese bombardment.

Japanese troops in Bataan.

A bombed-out settlement in Bataan.

Filipino scouts display a captured samurai sword.

Filipinos and Americans holding out on the Bataan peninsula.

Japanese artillery in action.

On 6 May 1942, realizing the position was hopeless, Wainwright offered to surrender. The Japanese refused to accept this until the guerilla forces still holding out on other parts of the island also gave up. Afraid of a massacre, Wainwright ordered a general surrender. Even so, some US guerillas continued to fight for another month, urged on by messages from MacArthur in Australia.

Wainwright surrenders to Homma.

By the end of the Philippines campaign, 30,000 Americans and 110,000 Filipino troops had been killed or captured, compared to 12,000 Japanese troops killed. General Homma was left with the task of finding leading Filipinos to help govern the country. Many refused, chief justice Jose Abad Santos among them: he was executed the day after Wainwright's surrender. The fate of the American and Filipino prisoners taken in Bataan and Corregidor was to be little better.

Left: Triumphant Japanese troops, Corregidor. **Above:** Wainwright broadcasts the surrender.

JAPANESE ATROCITIES

The Crimes of the Empire of the Sun

Within three months, Japan had broken the American blockade, taken control of the Dutch oil-fields and cowed the British Empire. It also now controlled all the world's rubber and 70 per cent of the world's tin. The 'Co-prosperity Sphere' was complete. It was an extraordinary military achievement.

But 'co-prosperity' was a propaganda word. "Burn up the whites in a blaze of victory," Japanese radio broadcasts exhorted local populations before their armies' arrival. Despite the rhetoric, the Japanese made the same mistake that the Germans had made in Russia. For while some indigenous peoples might have welcomed release from British, Dutch, French or American imperialism, their self-styled 'liberators' were primarily interested in their exploitation.

Even so, many local peoples at first believed Japanese propaganda. The Thai government made little objection to Japanese use of its territory to attack northern Malaya, and crowds greeted Japanese soldiers with flags and cheers in Java and Sumatra. Many Indian nationalists were prepared to fight under Japanese command against the British. In addition, Burma and the Philippines were granted nominal independence under Japanese 'protection', and in Indonesia the nationalist leader Achmed Sukarno, released from Dutch internment, worked with Japanese administrators to formulate an independent constitution.

A Japanese execution, China.

A brief respite on the Bataan Death March.

But these Japanese concessions to local self-rule were more apparent than real: the norm was institutionalized savagery.

If a Filipino forgot to bow three times to a Japanese soldier, he would be hanged from the nearest lamp post. In Sumatra, the Japanese carried out a violent suppression of the underground led by Amir Sjarifuddin: of those Sumatrans interned, nearly half had died by the end of the war. A further million Javanese and Sumatrans were used as forced labour to build the Burma railway, up to a third of them dying in the process. In 1943, when Chinese and other local prisoners revolted against the occupation in Jesselton, the capital of Borneo, hundreds of local villages were demolished and their inhabitants tortured. By the end of their first year in occupation, unimaginable cruelty had undermined nearly all support for the Japanese and left behind a legacy of bitterness which survives to this day.

The treatment of native populations in South-East Asia has perhaps been forgotten in the justified outrage over Japanese treatment of Western PoWs. Unlike the Nazis, the Japanese did not have a policy of genocide in their prison camps, but their behaviour had much the same effect. According to the Japanese military code of *bushido*, prisoners had surrendered all honour along with their freedom, and with honour had gone the right to humane consideration. The Japanese were astonished when American prisoners in Bataan asked for their names to be sent home so that their families would know they were alive. For the 'dishonour' of not fighting to the death, Western PoWs were regularly beaten,

LEFT AND ABOVE: American PoWs on the Death March.

399

A rest on the Death March.

starved, denied medical treatment, subjected to bizarre medical experiments or worked to death, while their Red Cross packages were looted. White men who refused to bow to Japanese soldiers received severe beatings – or worse. For the same offence, white women had their heads shaved.

No one was spared. Allied doctors were punished for letting their charges became weak and prone to disease on the meagre diet of 8 ounces of rice issued twice a day. Senior officers were given little more respect. The British governor of Hong Kong was imprisoned without contact with the world outside, then forced to work as a goatherd and beaten if the goats wandered. General Percival, who had signed the surrender in Singapore, was beaten for having dirt under his finger nails.

When the Japanese surrendered in 1945, 27 per cent of British and

ABOVE: US PoWs under guard. BELOW: Two Burmese bridges built by PoW labour.

Commonwealth prisoners had died in captivity, while 37 per cent of American PoWs had perished.

Branded on American and Filipino memories are the horrors that took place following the fall of Corregidor. Exhausted and starving prisoners were forced to march 60 miles in the blistering heat, without proper food or fresh water (Japanese guards would urinate in the brackish water before the prisoners drank) from Mariveles to San Fernando. Those who fell out of line, too tired to go on, were shot, bayoneted or left to die of dehydration. Between 10,000 and 16,000 prisoners never reached the end of the 'Bataan Death March'; in the first few weeks in the prison camps, another 16,000 Filipinos and 1000 Americans died.

For captured British and Australian troops, on the other hand, hell lay along the Burma Railway. Following their defeat at the Battle of Midway in June 1942, transport by sea was becoming increasingly difficult for the Japanese; they still needed to supply their Burmese offensive and this

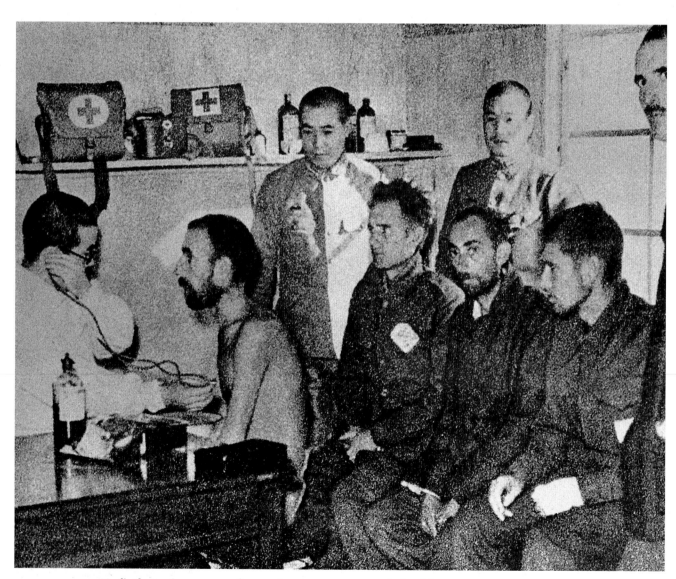

Medical care in a camp – from a Japanese propaganda booklet.

Distributing rations in a PoW camp.

A Japanese propaganda shot of a Christmas meal in a PoW camp (the meal was later removed).

Conditions inside a civilian internment camp.

Civilian internees suffering from beri-beri.

meant building an overland route between Bangkok and Rangoon. Any railway would have to cross thickly forested ravines and wind round mountains averaging 5000 feet in height: Japanese engineers estimated that, without heavy construction equipment, it would take up to five years to build. But the Japanese military command was in no mood for 'defeatism': it demanded that the line should be finished by the end of 1943. Nearly half of all the prisoners held by the Japanese in the region were used as slave labour on the railway – British, Australians, Dutch and a handful of Americans. Thousands of local people were also drafted in.

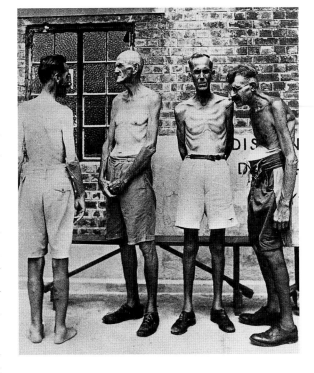

Day after day, prisoners were forced to get up before dawn and work flat out in the burning sun or – during the monsoon – rain and mud, returning only after dark to their ill-made, filthy huts. Weakened and badly-fed, they became increasingly susceptible to illness. Nearly 13,000 died in one cholera epidemic, and on one occasion guards tried to stem the outbreak by simply shooting the sick. The determination to build the railway

TOP AND ABOVE: Internees suffering from severe malnutrition.

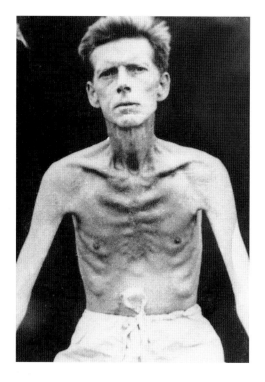

"can only be regarded as a cold-blooded, merciless crime against mankind, obviously premeditated," said an Australian doctor, Colonel Edward Dunlop, who witnessed these terrible events. The Burma-Thailand railway was indeed finished by 25 October 1943, but at the cost of 50,000 Allied prisoners. Up to a quarter of a million forced labourers from Burma, Java, Malaya, China and India also died.

Towards the end of the war, the Japanese, like the SS retreating through Russia, tried to cover up their war crimes. In December 1944, over 1600 maltreated Dutch, American and British prisoners were crammed below the decks of a ship to remove them from advancing American troops in the Philippines. Hundreds went mad with thirst, and when the ship was torpedoed and sunk, they were machine-gunned by Japanese in another ship. There were other horror stories. Up to 150 American prisoners on one Filipino island were ordered into deep air raid shelters before American troops arrived, and the shelters were set alight. Those who survived were beaten to death or buried alive. Similarly, when US troops landed on Palawan island to search for prisoners in February 1945, all they found were mass graves.

Top: A camp survivor. Above: The barracks of Changi Jail, Singapore.

Filipino refugees after liberation.

An American commando raid on one camp in Luzon rescued 500 PoWs just before they could be executed.

The outside world received little information about the Japanese treatment of PoWs (Red Cross inspectors were not allowed to visit in Japanese 'war zones'). The first reports of the Bataan Death March did not emerge until Spring 1943, and even then the true facts were held back for fear they would affect civilian morale.

Indeed, details of the most diabolical atrocities did not emerge until long after the war. In Manchuria, where the Japanese army had been in control since 1931, the 'Epidemic Prevention and Water Supply Unit' of the Kwantung army deliberately infected prisoners with fatal diseases as

Allied prisoners in Tokyo after liberation.

part of so-called medical research. In a series of horrific experiments, some were dissected or boiled alive while others were bombarded with lethal X-rays or given transfusions of horse blood.

Bitterness and anguish over Japanese wartime behaviour still exists both in China and the West. Survivors have been left with the task of giving the world uncomfortable reminders of the evils of the Empire of the Sun. "I have before me a list of 300 names of those PoWs who died on the tiny island of Haroekoem, in far western Indonesia," wrote a former prisoner in a letter to the London *Times* when Hirohito died in 1989. "Ragged and emaciated, they stumbled daily to build an airstrip, until abandonment of hope, or disease, brought them release. They died under unspeakable, degrading conditions. Pleas for help from the Red Cross, its patronage claimed by the Japanese Imperial Family, were ignored and the very mention of the Geneva Convention brought hysterical reaction. But we had surrendered and thus, in accordance with Japanese military custom, had forfeited all rights."

COUNTER-ATTACK

THE ALLIES HIT BACK
AT THE JAPANESE EMPIRE

GATHERING STRENGTH

The US War Machine Gears Up

The string of Japanese conquests in the Far East had been won at relatively low cost – 15,000 men, 380 aircraft and four destroyers. Speed had been vital, and now the Japanese strategy was to consolidate their gains before the US could recover sufficiently to mount a serious challenge in the Pacific. There was also the hope that a Nazi conquest of Russia would force America to the negotiating table. In the meantime, the Japanese navy's task was to make sure Australia and Hawaii were closed to American forces.

Huge resources were needed for that operation and, as the last pockets of Allied resistance were squeezed out of Burma and the Philippines,

Pressurized cabin-sections of new B-29s roll off the production line at the Boeing plant.

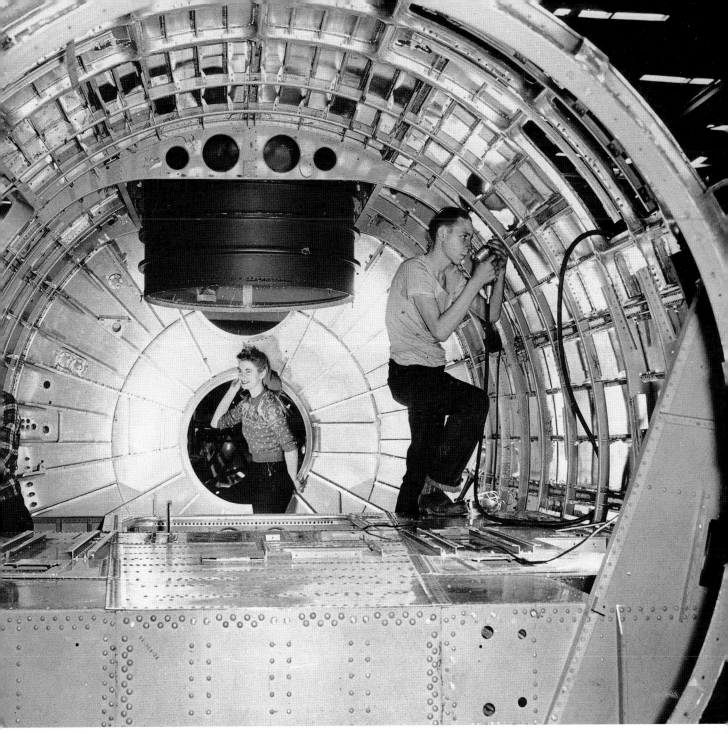

The nose sections of B-29s take shape.

there was debate in Tokyo about whether this would weaken the army in China. For though the Japanese army had triumphed elsewhere, it still faced constant attack from Mao's guerilla forces. The Japanese 'Three-All' campaign – 'kill all, burn all, destroy all'– had caused terrible hardship to the population but had little strategic impact in the vastness of China. The Communists were effectively mobilizing the peasantry and working behind Japanese lines in a way that the nationalists had signally failed to do.

Chiang himself sat in his capital of Chungking, avoiding decisive battles, waiting for Americans to deal with the Japanese on his behalf, and conserving his strength for the confrontation with Mao which he knew would follow at the end of the war. "The Japanese are a disease of the skin," he reasoned. "The Communists are a disease of the heart." But his régime was slowly disintegrating. Parts of China still under his control suffered from rampant inflation and corruption, as the wealthier classes were able to buy their way out of the army. Their places were filled by press gangs who dragged off anyone they could find. Many such civilians died of starvation in the long forced marches to join their units.

In the Pacific, time was growing short for the Japanese, who knew that America's enormous wealth was now being poured into the war effort. In the national fury after Pearl Harbor, Roosevelt announced plans to produce an astonishing 60,000 aircraft, 75,000 tanks and one million tons of merchant shipping each year. To meet the target, women were taken on in the factories while the men enlisted. One woman who worked on an aircraft line, nicknamed 'Rosie the Riveter', was used in a massive publicity campaign as the role model for a new generation of American women – tough and skilled but still feminine.

US battleships during exercises.

Nimitz on an inspection tour.

When MacArthur arrived in Australia, he was given the American Medal of Honour (America needed heroes at this low point of their war). But the American army awaiting his command in Australia was hardly up to his vision of an effective fighting force. There were only 26,000 troops and 260 planes: many of the former were half-trained, and many of the latter were in bad repair. MacArthur, a prickly character at the best of times, also deepened Allied divisions by refusing to include Australian or Dutch officers in his senior staff.

With ABDA disbanded, the new Allied command structure put the British in charge of Sumatra and the Indian Ocean area, while MacArthur took over the South-West Pacific and the new Pacific Fleet commander, Chester Nimitz, took over the Pacific Ocean proper. MacArthur and Nimitz had very different ideas. Since their commands overlapped, the result was almost constant disagreement about the dis-

Admiral 'Bull' Halsey on the bridge of a carrier.

Before the raid on Tokyo: Doolittle pins a medal to a bomb on the deck of the *Hornet,* April 1942.

ABOVE: Bombers on the flight deck of the *Hornet*. OPPOSITE: Take-off, 18 April 1942.

ABOVE: Naval air force commander Mitschner chats with Doolittle and his army fliers.

The cockpit and nose section of one of Doolittle's specially adapted Mitchells.

tribution of resources. "Of all the faulty decisions of the war, perhaps the most inexpressible was the failure to unify the command in the Pacific," wrote MacArthur later.

Harried by the Japanese propaganda broadcasts of 'Tokyo Rose', there was impatience in Washington to take revenge for Pearl Harbor and strike back at the heart of Japan. Since January 1942 this hazardous enterprise was being meticulously planned. If there was going to be an air raid on Tokyo, it would have to be launched from an aircraft carrier out of range of scout ships which patrolled up to 500 miles from the coast of Japan. That would mean a flight of 1100 miles – way beyond the limits of most naval aircraft. Not only this, but to spare the carriers the

Tokyo seen from one of Doolittle's planes.

Doolittle sits next to his plane, crash-landed in China.

After the raid: Doolittle's pilots in China.

danger of awaiting their return in enemy waters, they would have to fly on to China to refuel.

The solution which US naval aviation experts arrived at was to use specially adapted Mitchell bombers. Lt Colonel James Doolittle was chosen to lead the raid, and he and a band of top flyers set about practising the short take-offs they would need to leap into the air from the heaving deck of a carrier in the Pacific.

On 2 April, the aircraft carrier *Hornet* sailed from San Francisco with Doolittle and his 16 bombers on board, the carrier *Enterprise* in tow to provide fighter cover. On 18 April, still 650 miles away from Tokyo, the force was spotted by a Japanese patrol boat. Doolittle and the naval commander, Admiral Bill Halsey, decided that in spite of the extra distance it would be wise to take off as soon as possible. Four hours later, the bombers caught the air defences of Tokyo, Nagoya, Kobe, Yokohama and

The *Lexington* shortly before the end.

Survivors from the *Lexington* are pulled aboard a rescue ship.

The following day, both sides launched all-out attacks on each other's carriers. The *Lexington* was so badly hit that it sank five hours later. On the Japanese side, the *Shokaku* was seriously damaged. The two fleets then broke off the engagement.

Because of the loss of the *Lexington*, historians have called the Battle of the Coral Sea a stalemate. But though the Americans lost of one their precious carriers, the Japanese operation to take Port Moresby had to be abandoned. For the time being, Australia was safe.

The strength of the US fleet had shocked Yamamoto, who had expected the Americans to take much longer to recover their naval capacity following Pearl Harbor. He knew he must destroy the US Pacific Fleet once and for all while he had the advantage in naval power. The key to his plan was Midway Island, no more than a dot in the mid-Pacific. If this could

A Japanese raid on the Aleutian Islands.

June 1942: the aftermath of a Japanese raid on the Aleutians.

A Japanese transport ship in flames off the Aleutians.

be taken, its airstrip could be used to launch constant attacks against the US fleet. Secondly, Yamamoto expected the Americans to try to retake the island, and he hoped to ambush their carriers in the process.

Initially, the American fleet was to be lured north with an attack on the Aleutian Islands off the Alaskan coast. When the Americans arrived they were to be pinned down while Yamamoto and the Japanese fleet made for Midway. But once again the Americans were able to intercept the Japanese signals: Nimitz ignored the attack on the Aleutians and ordered the US fleet of three carriers and eight cruisers to Midway Island. Though the Americans had the advantage of surprise, their fleet was heavily outnumbered by the Japanese fleet of 11 battleships, eight

June 1942: bomb damage on Midway Island.

A damaged hanger on Midway Island.

A damaged Avenger torpedo bomber on Midway Island.

The comings and goings of US carrier planes during the Battle of Midway.

ABOVE: Repairing damage after Midway. BELOW: A flight of Avengers.

An Avenger damaged by flak.

carriers, 22 cruisers, and an enormous concentration of battleships, destroyers and submarines.

On 4 June, Japanese planes attacked Midway Island. Though much damage was caused, Yamamoto did not think it sufficient, and ordered a second strike. Meanwhile, the US carriers were waiting at a point 300 miles north of Midway. Admiral Fletcher in the *Yorktown* – its Coral Sea damage already repaired – ordered his planes to attack.

It was when the Japanese planes were at their most vulnerable, re-arming and re-fuelling on the flight decks, that the *Yorktown*'s planes struck. Ignited by direct hits, the bombs and petrol tanks of the Japanese planes on deck caused devastation and soon the carriers *Akagi, Kaga* and *Soryu* were consumed by raging infernos; the *Hiryu* was sunk later that day. When they realized it was too late, the crews transferred the portraits of the emperor to safety and abandoned ship. The captain of the *Soryu* stayed aboard, sword in hand, singing the national anthem as his ship went down.

Some Japanese planes had managed to get through the the wall of American flak and the flagship *Yorktown* was once again badly hit.

Dauntless dive-bombers in action.

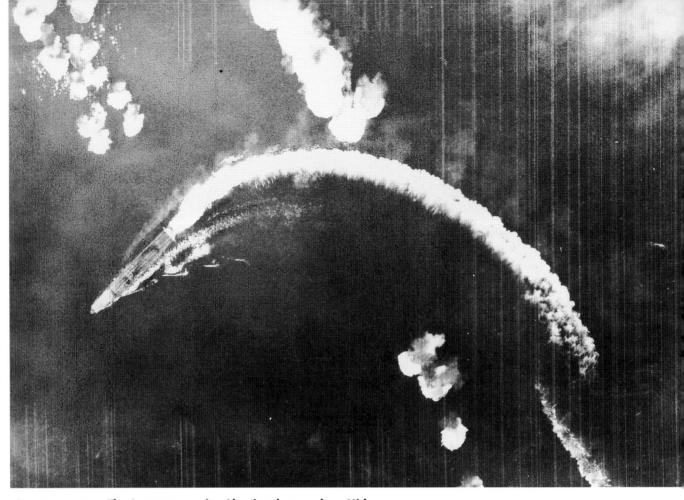

ABOVE AND BELOW: The Japanese carrier *Akagi* under attack at Midway.

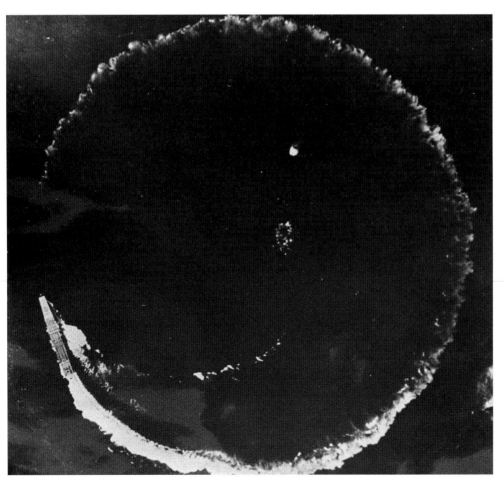

Tribespeople aiding Japanese troops in New Guinea.

Other tribesmen helping the Australians.

ABOVE AND BELOW: Allied supply lines run with local support in New Guinea.

American wounded in New Guinea.

Native scouts explaining the layout of Japanese positions to US troops.

An Australian mortar crew in action.

fer in the bloody battles for Guadalcanal in the Solomon Islands.

By the end of 1942, the Australian commander Sir Thomas Blamey, supplied by airdrops, had forced the Japanese back along the Buna peninsula. The Japanese had lost 12,000 troops in six months and when their last resistance ended on 21 January 1943, some preferred to swim out to sea to certain death rather than face the shame of capture.

Though prepared to help the Australians in New Guinea, in the early summer of 1942 MacArthur had been more preoccupied with battles in the US councils of war. After exhaustive negotiations, a compromise had been reached whereby Nimitz would command the first stage of an amphibious assault on the eastern Solomons, while MacArthur would take on the next two stages, capturing the rest of the Solomons as well as the New Guinea coast and the Bismarck Archipelago.

A tribesman getting medical help.

The Australians had set up a secret coast-watchers organisation of intelligence officers, planters and other volunteers on the islands of the region. On 5 July 1942 they reported that the Japanese were building an airstrip on the island of Guadalcanal. If it was finished, it would mean the Japanese air force could dominate the entire sector.

Guadalcanal is just 90 miles long by 25 miles wide, and is covered with thickly forested hills; its average rainfall of up to 200 inches a year is one of the heaviest in the world. But the island had to be the first American objective. Plans for its invasion were thrown together hurriedly, despite requests from some American commanders for a more gradual build-up.

The US landing fleet off Guadalcanal.

ABOVE AND OPPOSITE: US Marines bound for the Solomon Islands.

ABOVE AND BELOW: US reinforcements go ashore at Guadalcanal.

At 9am on 7 August 1942, after a heavy bombardment from the air and sea, 11,000 US marines waded ashore on Guadalcanal, while on nearby Tulagi, 6000 more wiped out Japanese resistance.

But Japanese commanders also realized the strategic importance of Guadalcanal – and they had a powerful naval force in the vicinity. It was ordered to attack. In the early hours of 8 August, cruisers under Admiral Guinichi Mikawa slipped through the narrow waters between the Solomon Islands and took the Allied ships by surprise. An hour later he withdrew leaving four Allied cruisers sinking and one badly damaged. This naval massacre became known as the Battle of Savo Island.

The US Marines on Guadalcanal were suddenly alone, without naval

An American light tank rumbles off the beach at Guadalcanal.

A B-17 bomber overflies the Solomon Islands.

Japanese marines on Guadalcanal.

September 1942: dead Japanese soldiers after the US victory on Guadalcanal.

US marine tanks grind through the jungle.

Hard-worked Marine stretcher-bearers.

or air support. For the next two weeks they were reduced to two meals a day, knowing that the Japanese now commanded the sea and air and that it would not be long before their troops arrived to reclaim the island. Radio Tokyo described the US Marines as "like the summer insects which have dropped into the fire by themselves".

Luckily for the Marines, the Japanese persistently underestimated the size of the force ranged against them. On 18 August, an advance party of just 1500 Japanese marines was landed: it was annihilated. The follow-up landing party was accompanied by a powerful naval force, including two battleships and three carriers. But the American admiral Robert Ghormley was warned of their approach and on 24 August his planes sank the Japanese carrier *Ryujo*.

More Japanese troops were being landed on the island by a shuttle of destroyers and landing ships known to the Marines as the 'Tokyo Express'. On the night of 13 September, the Marines found themselves battling desperately on what became known as Bloody Ridge. At one

US howitzers on the Guadalcanal front line.

ABOVE: US marines 'flushing out' snipers. BELOW: Fording a river on Guadalcanal.

US marines on the beach at Saipan.

Admiral's plane was shot down by American fighters. To hide the fact that they could break Japanese codes, the Americans did not announce the manner of Yamamoto's death, though they did report his funeral.

American command was still divided, however, with MacArthur pressing for his direct southern route to Japan and Nimitz and the US Navy wanting to use their growing carrier strength further north to exert pressure on various Japanese outposts. In May 1943, the so-called Trident Conference in Washington decided on a compromise – a two-pronged strategy that would force Japan to constantly switch reserves from one theatre to the other. But two 'prongs' meant double the effort and twice the preparation.

Before any other miltary venture, Roosevelt wanted to reassure American civilians by taking back the Aleutian islands near Alaska. On 11 May US Marines landed on Attu; two weeks of heavy fighting ensued

ABOVE AND BELOW: Marines advancing up the beach on Tarawa.

OPPOSITE: The aftermath of the battle for the island.

Dead Japanese at the entrance to their dugout, Tarawa.

ABOVE: Japanese dead on Saipan. BELOW: Medical aid for US wounded.

Burial service on board a US troop transport after the Saipan landings.

A prisoner appeals to comrades to surrender.

Japanese civilians sheltering in a cave.

Five days without water: Japanese civilians come out of hiding on Saipan.

Tinian Island under US bombardment.

US marines come ashore on Tinian.

US artillerymen on a vantage point, Tinian.

General Edson on Tinian.

July 1944: US Marines arrive on Guam.

Pushing through Guam.

US troops push forwards on Guam.

and Admiral Nagumo (who had led the Pearl Harbor strike force) committed suicide. They hoped this would "encourage the troops in their final attack".

An immense slaughter followed. Those Japanese soldiers who did not die in battle committed suicide; a few hundred Japanese soldiers swam out to the coral reefs, where one officer was seen beheading his men. In the days that followed, as many as 22,000 Japanese civilians also killed themselves in the island caves to avoid capture.

On 18 July, Saipan fell. In Japan there was no one to blame for the loss of the island but Tojo, who had concentrated all military and government power in his own hands. He was forced to resign as prime minister.

On 23 July, the Marines shifted their attention to Tinian and Guam. On Tinian they watched in horror as Japanese soldiers queued to leap to their deaths from cliffs, or blew themselves up with hand grenades. Only after the soldiers had disposed of themselves did the remaining 13,000 Japanese civilians surrender. By the middle of August 1944, the Marianas were in American hands. The next great task was to retake the Philippines.

A Japanese prisoner on Guam.

THE BATTLE FOR BURMA

British and Commonwealth Triumphs

By May 1942, when the remains of the British and Chinese armies defending Burma had been forced back to the Indian border, the reputation of the Japanese as invincible jungle fighters was at an all-time high. The British Empire had been dealt a shattering blow with the loss of Singapore; the next great imperial possession in the sights of the Japanese was India, where they hoped to capitalize on nationalist disaffection. In April 1943, the Indian leader, Subhas Chandra Bose, began to build an Indian National Army in Burma to fight alongside the Japanese. Within a year, 25,000 Indian prisoners in Japanese camps had volunteered to fight the British – though many were later to desert.

The first British counter-attack in Burma, known as the First Arakan

Japanese troops in Burma.

Gurkhas in Arakan prepare to attack a Japanese patrol.

offensive, was pushed back by the Japanese at Donbaik in December 1942. British and Indian troops were hampered by new weapons, many of which were found to be faulty, and found progress through the thick jungle painfully slow. There was also the problem of disease on an epidemic scale. Within a month of the offensive, 40 per cent of troops were suffering from malaria. Many died from infected cuts (even shaving was hazardous). Allied morale was further weakened by stories of the brutal Japanese treatment of prisoners – in particular their practice of tying men to trees in the line of fire.

Plainly the British needed to reorganize their command and restore morale. The mercurial Admiral Lord Louis Mountbatten was chosen to be the region's new commander-in-chief. At 42, Mountbatten was one of the youngest and brightest of Allied war leaders.

British artillery on the Arakan front.

Lord Mountbatten.

Punjab troops fight a village fire in Arakan.

British troops prepare a cook-up in the Arakan jungle.

March 1942: Indian troops on the offensive in Arakan.

A Japanese prisoner watched over by a Sikh MP.

Mountbatten took over in August 1943, with the American Stilwell as his deputy. Their problems were many. The forces under their command comprised British, Indians, Gurkhas, Americans, Dutch, French, Australians, New Zealanders and Chinese, and food and medical supplies were short. The Burma campaign was a matter of three words, said Mountbatten – "Morale, Monsoon, Malaria". He brought a wry humour to his dealings with the battered army. "I hear you call yourselves the Forgotten Army," he told the troops. "Well, let me tell you, you are not the Forgotten Army. In fact, nobody has even heard of you."

Restoring morale meant demonstrating that the Japanese could be defeated. Jungle operations in Burma were already in progress when

Wingate and his Chindits.

ABOVE AND BELOW: Indian army regulars in action.

ABOVE: Sick and wounded Chindits after their first operation.

Mountbatten arrived. Under the Englishman, Orde Wingate, and the American, Colonel Merrill, guerilla activities were being carried out behind the Japanese lines. In February 1943, 3000 of Wingate's Chindits (named after a mythical Burmese animal called a *chinthe*) crossed the Chindwin for their first morale-boosting expedition. Though nearly a quarter of them were never to return, the Chindits' exploits had so impressed Churchill that their numbers were tripled and Wingate was given his own air unit – known as 'Cochran's Circus' after their American commander, Philip Cochran. During the next offensive, five Chindit brigades were airlifted into Burma and successfully cut Japanese communication and supply routes.

At the end of 1943, General Slim was ready to move back into Arakan. But the Japanese realized that the build-up of troops and equipment signalled a renewed offensive, and decided to strike first. They marched directly into India.

It was clear that the Japanese counter-offensive was aimed at two strongpoints – Imphal and Kohima. The latter was defended by just 1500 British and Indian troops, and in early 1944 they were entirely cut off. On 18 March reinforcements managed to break through to the garrison just as it was about to make its last stand.

Chindits cross a river in occupied Burma.

Stilwell celebrates his birthday.

Merrill's Marauders on the march.

Merrill's Marauders pick their way through the jungle.

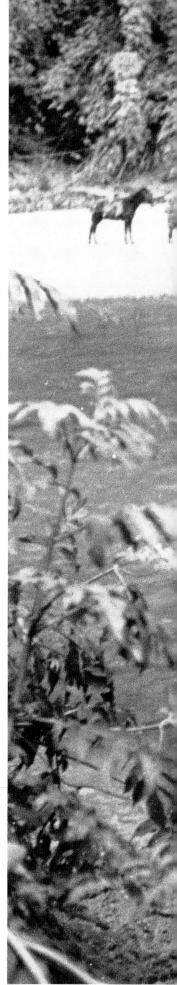

Merrill's Marauders crossing into Burma from Assam.

US regulars crossing the Chindwin River in northern Burma.

British troops near Kohima.

Mountbatten now took a risk and flew in more reserves, determined to hold on to the cities and knowing that, as the Japanese had less than 200 planes in Burma, he could now rely on command of the air. Even though Imphal was also surrounded, Allied planes kept it supplied and flew out civilians and wounded. As the seige dragged on, Japanese forces under General Renya Mutaguchi became increasingly exposed. But he sacked three subordinates when they urged him to withdraw – only to be replaced himself by a new commander.

British and Indian troops meet on the Imphal-Kohima road.

Indian sappers and miners clear a barricaded bridge.

Gurkha troops clearing the road from Imphal to Kohima.

American troops relaxing in Burma just 75 yards from Japanese positions.

A British officer takes a 'breather' near Kohima.

March 1945: Australian troops take Meiktila, 80 miles south of Mandalay.

When Kohima and Imphal were relieved in July 1944 they had withstood an 88-day siege. Outside the defences the Japanese had suffered atrocious hardship: 65,000 were found dead – some 40,000 from starvation or disease. The Allied victory signalled the end of Japanese designs on the subcontinent.

New medical advances in the fight against malaria, and Mountbatten and Stilwell's determination to fight through the next monsoon (despite most military advice), meant that Allied troops were now both better prepared and motivated. Though Wingate had died in an air crash on 24 March, Merrill's Marauders continued to mount daring raids over the mountains, capturing the vital airfield of Myitkyina. In the summer, British, Indian, Gurkha and American troops took Mogaung, the first town inside Burma. The slow and bloody Japanese retreat from South-East Asia had begun.

The US naval task force near Leyte.

Kurita's fleet makes for Leyte.

transfer to the battleship *Yamato*, generally regarded as unsinkable.

Though some Japanese naval pilots were so inexperienced that they were unable to land on their carriers, they did succeed in turning the US fast carrier *Princeton* into an inferno. The American response was devastating. On 24 October, as many as 250 sorties against the main Japanese fleet sank the massive battleship *Musashi*. "We had expected air attacks," said one senior Japanese officer, "but this day's were almost enough to discourage us."

Nonetheless, the Japanese trap was working. Confused by the reports of his own pilots, Halsey went with his whole carrier fleet to destroy the Japanese decoy force under Ozawa. MacArthur's invasion fleet was left

The US battleship *Pennsylvania* bombards Leyte.

Setting up anti-aircraft positions on Leyte Island.

LSTs disgorge their troops on Leyte Beach.

Admiral Kincaid.

almost undefended during the night. As Halsey dashed northwards on 25 October, another portion of the Japanese fleet was cornered in traditional naval style by six US battleships and destroyed.

When dawn broke on 26 October, Kurita's main attacking force was six hours behind schedule but still intact. Neither Halsey nor Kincaid, who commanded the landing support ships, realized that the entrance to the vital San Bernardino Strait was open. When Kurita crept through, he could see the invasion fleet laid out before him and defended only by a small force of warships under Admiral Clifton Sprague.

The Americans, panicking, had also sighted Kurita. "Prepare to attack major portion of Japanese Fleet," signalled the commander of the US destroyer *Johnston*, which sank a large Japanese cruiser with torpedoes before it was sunk in turn. From behind a smokescreen, fierce US resistance was enough to convince Kurita that the force opposing him was much bigger than it really was. Believing he was risking his ships, he turned away from the Gulf. "I could not believe my eyes," said Sprague. "It took a whole series of reports from circling planes to convince me."

Halsey, meanwhile, had destroyed all four Japanese carriers in the decoy force under Ozawa, and was receiving a string of increasingly desperate pleas for help back in Leyte Gulf. He realized he would have to

Sprague watches the progress of the landings.

Admiral Kurita.

A Japanese battleship under air attack.

Repairing *kamikaze* damage on the US carrier *Sewanee*.

The USS *Missouri* seconds before a *kamikaze* hit.

Fire-hoses playing over the USS *Princeton*.

A *kamikaze* hits the US carrier *St Lo*.

511

An American naval pilot waits before an air strike.

The magazine of a Japanese destroyer explodes.

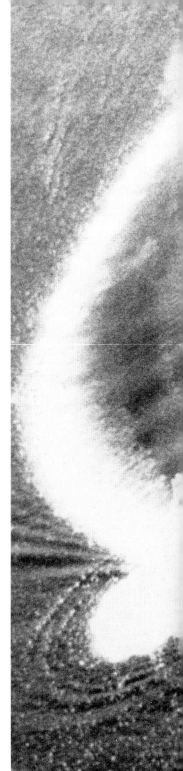

A Japanese cruiser takes evasive action.

turn away before he could get his battleships within range of the Japanese admiral himself. "At that moment, Ozawa was exactly 42 miles from the muzzles of my 16-inch guns," he wrote later. "I turned my back on the opportunity I had dreamed of since my days as a cadet."

In the Leyte engagements, the Japanese navy had lost three battleships, four large carriers and nine cruisers. Its capacity to inflict severe damage on the US Pacific Fleet was gone forever.

On the island itself, monsoon meant that it was the end of November before the new airstrips were dry enough to use. Once they were, the

November 1944: *kamikaze* damage to the cruiser *St Louis*.

Americans had to fight off a series of parachute drops to regain them. By 10 December, US troops had taken the city of Ormoc, where only 15,000 Japanese troops out of the original 65,000 were left alive. On Christmas Day, 1944, MacArthur announced the end of organized resistance on Leyte, though mopping-up operations were to continue for many months afterwards.

Without Leyte, the Japanese knew they could not hold the Philippines; and without the Philippines, their supply lines had been cut to the oilfields in the East Indies. In desperation they resorted to the *kamikazes*, or suicide pilots.

Opposite: **Japanese ships under attack in Manila Bay.**

Kamikazes (named after the 'divine wind' which rescued Japan from the Mongol invasion fleet in 1281) appeared for the first time against American carriers defending the Leyte landings. On the day of their mission, *kamikaze* pilots were told they were "already gods without earthly desires" and given white *hachimaki* headbands like the samurai of old. Then, after a ceremonial toast to the emperor, they were sent off in obsolete planes packed with high explosive. The object was simply to break through defensive flak and crash into their target.

The first *kamikaze* victim was the escort carrier *St Lo*; the crash ignited the torpedoes and ammunition below decks and in the ensuing explosion the carrier sank and a number of nearby ships were seriously damaged. By the end of 1944, the havoc wrought on the US Navy had become so extensive that MacArthur and Nimitz ordered a news black-out – both to prevent panic back home and to make sure the Japanese were not

American howitzers on Leyte Island.

ABOVE AND BELOW: US troops pounding the Japanese near the Burma Road.

LEFT: The first convoy along the Burma Road.

ABOVE AND OPPOSITE: General Lewis Pick at the head of the first Burma Road convoy.

linked up with their compatriots from China itself at Mongyu, and the following day the first 500 lorries made the journey through from Burma. Despite his bitter personal battles with his former chief of staff, Chiang renamed the route the Stilwell Road.

Meanwhile, Slim's plan to encircle the Japanese at Mandalay was beginning to take effect. When British and Indian troops marched into the town on 20 March, the remaining Japanese troops realized they were in danger of being cut off and were forced to retreat.

But Rangoon was still over 300 miles away, and Slim desperately needed a port in the south of Burma before his supply chain broke down. Mountbatten came to his aid, ordering amphibious and parachute landings at the mouth of the Rangoon river. On 2 May, Allied planes saw that prisoners of war in the city had painted on their roof the words: "Japs gone. Exdigitate". Troops moved quickly upriver and duly found the city

The US and Chinese in ruined Lashio.

US bombers cut Japanese supply routes.

Chinese troops in northern Burma.

The road to Mandalay: British troops on the outskirts.

Fighting in the heart of Mandalay.

THE TOKYO FIRESTORMS

The US Bombing Campaign against Japan

In Europe, the British bomber commander Sir Arthur Harris had made his mark with his determination to end the war by air bombing alone. In the Pacific from 1943 onwards, Harris had an American equivalent, General Curtis LeMay. LeMay not only believed that Japan could be bombed into submission, he was also sure that, in the Boeing B-29 Superfortress, he had the weapon to do it.

The Superfortress was designed specifically for bombing missions over Japan. Each aircraft had a range of 5000 miles, weighed 60 tons and was designed to carry 2000 pounds of bombs; the crew flew at heights of up

Superfortresses over Mount Fuji.

General Curtis LeMay next to a B-29 engine cowling.

Bombs ready for loading.

against the Musashina engine factory. Though the mission was ineffective, mass formation flying proved that losses could be drastically reduced. By March 1945, raids on Japan regularly comprised 300 bombers whose combined defensive firepower posed a serious threat to Japanese fighters. Escorting Mustangs also shot down their slower opponents by the score.

LeMay's 'accuracy' problem was twofold: the enormous fuel-load needed by B-29s to fly to Japan and back limited the number of bombs they could carry, and at 30,000 feet the crews were unable to pinpoint the 'cottage industry' style of Japanese production. His solution was to save fuel and increase bomb loads by ordering a series of lower-altitude incendiary raids on cities. Crews would forget pinpoint targets and instead devastate wide areas by deliberately causing firestorms.

June 1945: A firebomb raid on Kobe.

US ordnance teams keep the stock high.

Changing the engine of a B-29 in India.

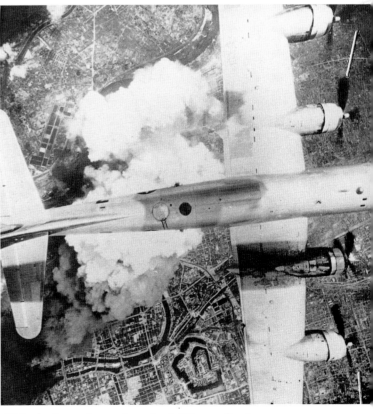

Oil leaks from the engine of a B-29 over Osaka.

The air gunner's view of a B-29 trip over Japan.

A Japanese cruiser under air attack in port.

This raid destroyed nearly seven square miles of Yokohama.

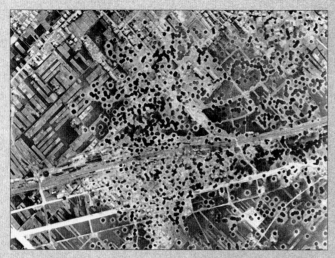

The Marifu rail yards after attack by B-29s.

Razed to the ground: the Mitsubishi plant in Nagoya.

All that remained of a section of Tokyo.

Tokyo after a devastating firestorm.

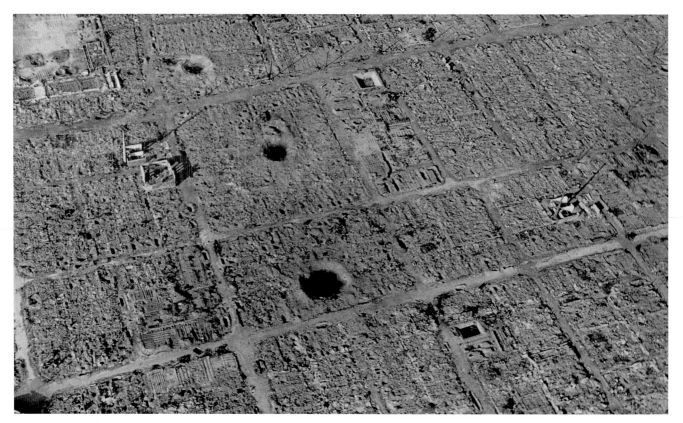

Part of Osaka levelled by B-29 attack.

ized that enormous suffering had been caused to civilians, they were hardened by stories of Japanese atrocities. It seemed an acceptable price to pay to ease the US landings on Japan, which still seemed imminent.

By 19 March, having dropped 10,000 tons of bombs on Osaka, Kobe and Nagoya, the B-29s had run out of incendiaries and attacks had to be suspended. But in July the raids were renewed with threefold intensity. Civilian morale now seemed to be truly shattered, for when LeMay dropped leaflets warning where the B-29s were going to bomb next, over eight million people left for the countryside, seriously disrupting Japanese war production.

The raids proved that Japan was all but defenceless. The US airforce had almost complete command of the air, and sustained only fractional losses. From February 1945, Allied navy pilots had even begun raiding Japanese factories from carriers steaming just 175 miles off the coast. For Japan's leaders there seemed to be no hope – only a willingness to risk complete annihilation.

A Japanese civilian inspects the wreckage of his home.

BLACK SAND

The Landings on Iwo Jima and Okinawa

The small volcanic island of Iwo Jima is only 660 miles from Tokyo. It is not a pleasant place. In fact, the reporter John Lardner described it as "a miserable piece of real estate… with no water, few birds, no butterflies, no discernible animal life – nothing but sand and clay, humpbacked hills, stunted trees, knife-edged kuna grass in which mites who carry typhus live, and a steady, dusty wind." Yet as early as September 1943, when their bombing campaign against Japan got underway, the Americans realized that the island would be vital for airstrips for the B-29s' escorts.

Iwo Jima's proximity to Japan meant that it was heavily defended. Being only five miles long and, at the widest point, two and a half miles wide, it was also relatively easy to fortify. Lack of cover would make its conquest a perilous and costly business.

February 1945: Mount Suribachi with LSTs on the beach.

US naval planes on their way to support marines on Iwo Jima.

For 72 days at the end of 1944, the US navy and air force pulverized the island's defences in the longest and heaviest bombardment of the Pacific War. On 19 February 1945, as many as 450 invasion ships arrived offshore. Forty five minutes after the first landing craft set off in the 4000-yard dash to the beaches, the first seven Marine battalions under 'Howling Mad' Smith were ashore.

When they were no more than 300 yards inland, the Marines were greeted by a withering defensive fire. Mortars raked up and down the black beaches; US troops huddled for cover in the shellholes. The next three weeks saw some of the most bitter fighting of the Pacific War.

It took three days for Marines to struggle up to the peak of the volcano Suribachi on the tip of the island, and raise the Stars and Stripes. By 9 March, they had reached the other end of the island and Smith ordered 'mopping-up' operations. But the battle was far from over. The remains

Japanese planes burning after an air strike on Iwo Jima.

of the island had been turned into a vast network of fortified tunnels, manned by troops who had each sworn to kill at least ten American soldiers before they were themselves killed. "Have not eaten or drunk for five days," wrote the Japanese commander, General Tadamichi Kuribayashi on 15 March. "But fighting spirit is running high. We are going to fight bravely to the last moment."

He was proved right: only 1083 of the 23,000 Japanese troops defending Iwo Jima were taken prisoner, while nearly 7000 US Marines were killed. Twenty four US Medals of Honor were awarded.

Before fighting had ended, the first US bombers had landed on the island. On 7 April, the first Mustangs took off from it to escort a daylight air raid on Tokyo. Three months after the battle, as many as 850 US

US amphibious craft circle a battleship on their way to the beaches.

Kamikaze damage on the US carrier *Saratoga.*

US Hellcat fighters with the landing fleet in the distance.

Marines under fire on the slopes of Mount Suribachi.

A US artillery position.

Mass on the summit of Mount Suribachi, with Marines shielding the 'altar' from the wind.

Joe Rosenthal's Pulitzer Prize-winning photograph of Marines planting the Stars and Stripes on top of Mt Suribachi.

Japanese dead on Iwo Jima.

B-29s on the Iwo Jima airfield.

bombers had made emergency landings on Iwo Jima. Had the island not been taken, they would probably have crashed into the sea.

Yet the ferocity of the fighting on Iwo Jima rattled US chiefs of staff: if the battle for a tiny island near Japan had cost so many lives, what would it mean to invade Japan itself?

Like Iwo Jima, the island of Okinawa – the next US target up the Japanese island chain – was volcanic. It was also 67 miles long and honeycombed with caves. American planners realized grimly that the battle to take it could be their toughest yet.

The task was given to the 170,000 troops of the US Tenth Army under General Simon Buckner. Operation Iceberg, as it was designated, got underway with another massive bombardment from air and sea starting on 25 March 1945. For the first time, the Americans were joined in the Pacific by the British fleet, and the steel decks of the British carriers were tested to the limit by *kamikaze* attacks. Both the British and Americans

US battleships bombard the beaches of Okinawa.

ABOVE AND BELOW: *Kamikaze* attacks on US carriers off Okinawa.

Briefing Japanese *kamikaze* pilots.

had developed techniques to deal with the *kamikazes*, posting anti-aircraft ships at a distance from the main fleet to knock out the suicide planes before they could get close to their targets. Nonetheless, *kamikazes* succeeded in causing enormous damage: 5000 US naval personnel were killed by the 350 suicide missions launched during the landings. Even the Japanese flagship *Yamato* was sent out on a suicide mission. But after a two-hour attack from US dive-bombers on 7 April, it was sunk without ever having used its enormous guns against an enemy target.

The Okinawa landings began on 1 April. The whole operation soon developed into a larger re-run of Iwo Jima. Once again the invaders encountered little opposition as they hit the beaches, only to come up against entrenched Japanese positions in the interior; once again, resistance was fanatical, to-the-death. Hand-to-hand fighting was frequent and the Japanese launched numerous suicide attacks. No mercy was asked and none given. Almost all captured US troops were killed by the Japanese; in return the Americans used flame-throwers to 'flush' defenders out of the island's caves.

American losses in the three month battle were heavy: 12,500 dead (included Buckner himself). Japanese casualties, on the other hand, were simply staggering: nearly 110,000 troops died, and another 75,000 civilians were killed by the constant US bombardment or in the soldiers' crossfire. And Okinawa had another dimension of tragedy. Hundreds of Japanese civilians jumped to their deaths from the island's steep cliffs rather than become prisoners, and many others, including 85 Japanese

ABOVE: A US patrol sets out for the interior, Okinawa. BELOW: A Sherman flame-thrower in action.

A Marine using a flame-thrower to 'flush out' a cave on Okinawa.

Infantry hitch a ride, Okinawa.

A US army cook bravely samples his own food.

A rare Japanese surrender on Okinawa.

student nurses who hid in a cavern now revered as the 'Cave of the Virgins', were killed by GIs who mistook them for Japanese troops.

When the Americans finally managed to fight their way into the Japanese headquarters cave at Naha, they found that the 200 wounded soldiers and senior officers inside had killed themselves. The leaders of the Japanese forces on Okinawa, generals Ushijima and Sho, committed suicide on 22 June. "I depart without regret, shame or obligations," said Sho in his final message.

The surviving 10,000 Japanese soldiers turned themselves into guerilla units of 200 men each, sharing rifles and eking out ammunition. But on the night of 14 August, the Japanese saw something extraordinary from their hideouts: the fireworks of the Allied fleet spelling 'Victory' to mark the end of the war. At first they refused to believe it. But in the days that followed they slowly emerged, hollow-faced and exhausted – some 7400 ready to endure, as their emperor put it, "the unendurable": defeat.

ABOVE AND OPPOSITE: The very different reactions of Japanese and US troops at the end of hostilities.

THE A-BOMB

The Destruction of Hiroshima and Nagasaki

An oil embargo had precipitated the Pacific War, and by mid-1945 it was the Japanese oil shortage that was bringing it to a close. Supplies from the Dutch East Indies were simply not getting through: the blockade by Allied submarines had proved highly effective. In fact, so much of the Japanese merchant fleet had been sunk by the beginning of the year that American submarines were being diverted to pick up the crews of ditched Allied aircraft.

Without enough fuel to run what little remained of their fleet and air

ABOVE: The mushroom cloud over Nagasaki. OPPOSITE: Captain Tibbets takes off on the Hiroshima mission.

Fathers of the bomb: Einstein and Oppenheimer.

force, Japanese imperial command could do little more than watch the destruction of their country by Allied ships and planes. With Okinawa all but taken and the invasion of the mainland imminent, they also began to fear that growing disaffection and defeatism might bring about a Communist takeover.

Over the previous six months, the Japanese 'thought police' had been more active than ever tracking down rumour-mongers and anonymous letter-writers. Hirohito himself was sent a stream of angry cards: one postcard from a 12-year-old boy read simply, "Stupid Emperor". Faced with increasing social chaos, in February 1945 prime minister Fumimaro urged Hirohito to surrender quickly and save the country from revolution.

Meanwhile, 2.4 million Japanese had been called up to defend their homeland and sent to lodge with unwilling villagers in the countryside. Even before the air raids began, absenteeism from the factories ran at 20 per cent. Now 51 per cent of all homes had been destroyed by the bombs, and another 13 per cent blown up to make firebreaks. Food was strictly

The Potsdam Conference, July 1945.

Final briefing for the crew of 'Enola Gay'.

rationed: each person was allowed no more than 1200 calories a day.

Allied military planners who had made such a success of D-Day were carefully developing plans for the invasion of Japan, and MacArthur was estimating another one million casualties before the country would surrender – an event he predicted for the winter of 1946. But the next stage in the approach to Japan, the invasion of Kyushu planned for November 1945, would never happen.

On 5 April, after the news of the American landings on Okinawa, the elderly Admiral Kantaro Suzuki had became prime minister. He was already 78, and he faced a hard job. If he talked of peace too openly, he risked a military coup; unless he did so, the destruction would continue. Suzuki re-appointed as foreign minister Shigenori Togo, who had been living in retirement since the failure of his efforts to avoid war in 1941.

But even the peace party were determined to keep Hirohito on the throne: there had to be some way to get round the Allied demand for unconditional surrender. Suzuki's mistake – against Togo's advice – was to put out peace feelers to Stalin first, in the hope that he would act as intermediary. But Stalin had his eye on Far-Eastern gains, and he reject-

The crew of 'Enola Gay' before the raid on Hiroshima.

ed these overtures. Nonetheless, by intercepting Suzuki's messages to his ambassador in Moscow, the Allies knew there was a good chance that dropping their insistence on unconditional surrender would persuade the emperor to overrule his cabinet.

In fact the Japanese cabinet remained divided even after 20 June, when Emperor Hirohito had summoned the Supreme War Direction Council and told them: "You will consider the question of ending the war as soon as possible." Three were in favour of immediate unconditional surrender, but the army minister and chiefs of staff still wanted some conditions attached.

By now Roosevelt had died, and had been replaced by Harry Truman. The Americans had begun to share Churchill's deep distrust of Stalin; at the Potsdam Conference in July, Allied chiefs of staff were increasingly nervous about Stalin's promised entry into the Pacific theatre.

And there was another consideration: the atomic bomb which the USA and Britain had been struggling to develop was nearly ready. Churchill and Truman were planning to warn Stalin off interference in the East as soon as they knew the result of the crucial first nuclear test, which was to take place at Alamagordo, New Mexico.

On 17 July, Truman arrived at Potsdam to receive a cryptic message. "Operated on this morning," it began. "Diagnosis not yet complete, but

Final instructions before the flight.

results seem satisfactory, and already exceed expectations." Churchill received a similar note reading "babes satisfactorily born". The world's first nuclear test had been a success.

At this point, Churchill returned to Britain for the results of the general election, and found that he had lost. He was replaced at Potsdam by his own former deputy, Clement Attlee. The conference ended by issuing a stern warning to the Japanese government, urging them to surrender or face complete destruction. The bomb was not mentioned.

Suzuki's ambivalent reply to the warning constituted his second seri-

Attlee: replaced Churchill at Potsdam.

ous mistake. He said he would "withhold comment on" the warning: this was translated for Truman as 'ignore'.

At the same time, foreign minister Togo was sending an urgent message to his Moscow ambassador: "Since the loss of one day relative to this present matter may result in a thousand years of regret, it is requested that you immediately have a talk with Molotov". But Vyacheslav Molotov, Stalin's foreign minister, delayed the talk: Soviet forces were preparing to invade Manchuria.

By late July, time had already run out for the Japanese: Truman had made up his mind "to shorten the agony of the war". The A-bomb had been delivered to Tinian Island by the US cruiser *Indianapolis*. In the early hours of 6 August, after three days waiting for the weather to clear, the B-29 'Enola Gay' took off from a specially lengthened runway. In its bomb-bay was the A-bomb codenamed 'Little Boy'.

On board were four hand-picked scientists and a crew of nine captained by Paul Tibbets. Just after 8am they could see the city of Hiroshima ahead, and put on protective arc-welder's goggles.

The bomb was dropped just after 8.15am. Fifty-one seconds later it exploded less than 2000 feet above the city. Now 15 miles away, Tibbets could see an immense ball of fire, then the tell-tale mushroom cloud.

'Enola Gay' on the tarmac.

ABOVE AND TOP: 'Little Boy' and its effect on Hiroshima.

'A-Bomb Dome' – one of few buildings left standing by the Hiroshima blast.

LEFT: Site of a vaporized A-bomb victim. ABOVE: Japanese troops at Hiroshima railway station.

Back in Guam – the crew of 'Enola Gay'.

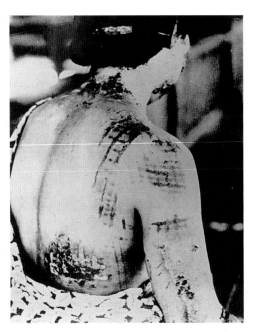

Kimono pattern burned into skin.

"The surface was nothing but a black, boiling ... barrel of tar," he said. "Where before there had been a city – distinctive houses, buildings and everything that you could see from our altitude – now you couldn't see anything except black boiling debris down below."

In seconds, the A-bomb's fireball had vaporized thousands of people in the city, leaving their shadows scorched into walls. Tens of thousands more were horribly burned. The shockwave which followed – a force of eight tons per square yard – flattened buildings, tore clothes and skin from bodies, and wiped out the city's entire commercial and residential centre. Between 71,000 and 80,000 people were killed instantly by the blast; estimates of total dead, including those from radiation, range from 160,000 to 240,000.

The people of Hiroshima had in general been spared by the fire-raids, but expected one imminently. For weeks they had been queuing up with their carts to leave the city. Even so, when the bomb was dropped the population was still 300,000.

Three days after Hiroshima had been razed to the ground, a second

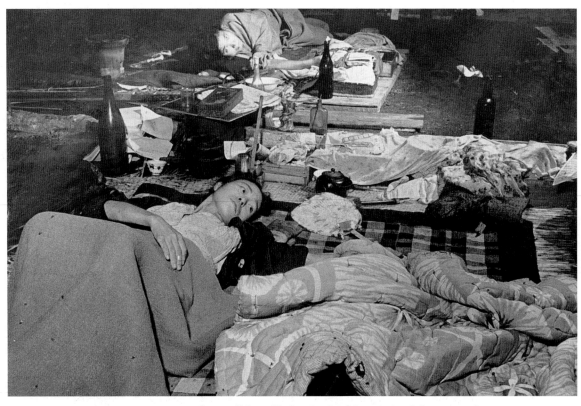

ABOVE AND OPPOSITE: The terrible suffering in the aftermath of the A-Bomb.

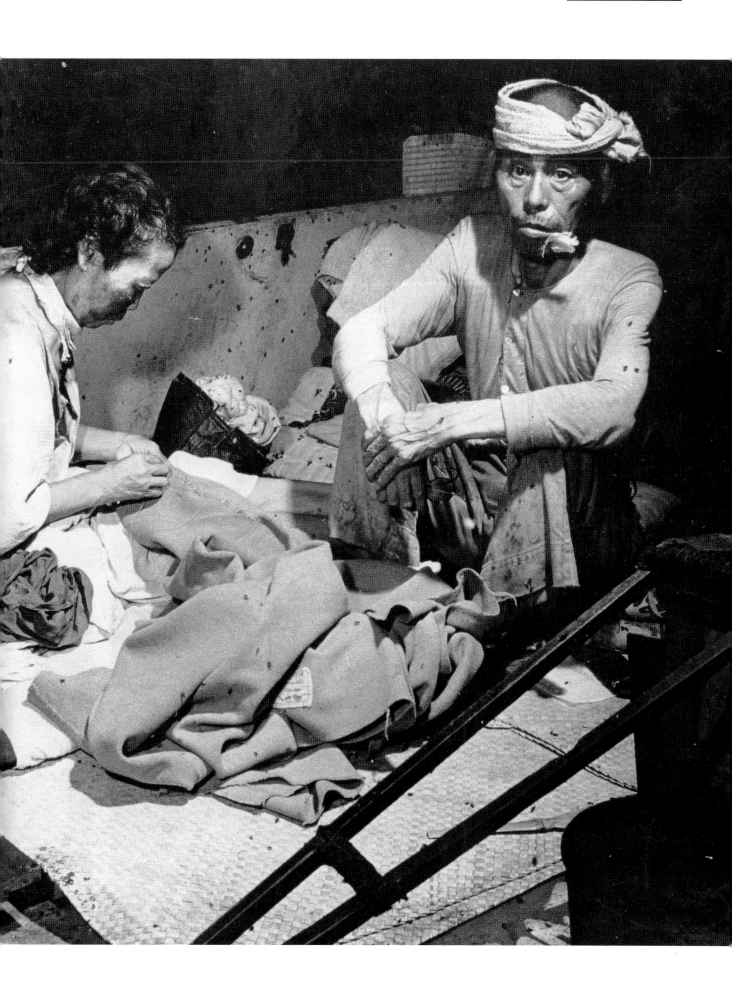

The Bomb's epicentre, Nagasaki.

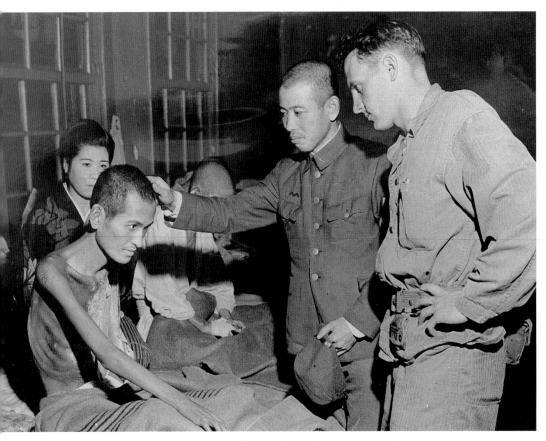

US Navy experts are shown the effects of flash burns, Nagasaki.

Bitter taste of defeat: a German soldier in the rubble of Berlin.

Washington and Moscow. The old colonial empires of the British, French and Dutch, on the other hand, were beginning to collapse. In the Far East, where the Japanese had portrayed themselves as liberators, the effect of their defeat was ironically to end the grip of imperialism. Three years after the war, India was partitioned and given independence under Mountbatten's guidance. Malaya, Java and Sumatra, Burma and Indo-China faced periods of political upheaval and civil strife before they achieved independence.

With the exception of America – which was richer than ever – most countries were bankrupt by the end of hostilities. At least $1 trillion had been spent on waging war, $272 million by Germany alone. Not only was Germany bankrupt, it faced the task of clearing some five billion cubic

ABOVE: The beginnings of reconstruction. BELOW: Hungry Berliners gaze into a butcher's shop.

1948: supplies arrive during the Berlin Airlift.

Japanese troops on their way home.

yards of rubble – all that remained of its historic cities. To tackle this immense problem, in 1947 General George Marshall introduced his enlightened aid plan to help rebuild the shattered economies of western Europe and Japan. The Marshall Plan was rejected by Stalin, however, and he made sure none of the other Eastern bloc leaders accepted it.

By VE-Day, the transition between war in Europe and the armed stand-off of the Cold War was almost complete. "From Stettin in the Baltic to Trieste in the Adriatic, an Iron Curtain has descended across the continent," Churchill warned in a speech in Missouri, and in the new atomic world this was a dangerous division. For the next half century, an uneasy peace reigned under the shadow of the A-bomb. The opportunity for peace without fear in Europe did not finally emerge until the destruction of the Berlin Wall in 1989. Even then, the ethnic hatreds which the Nazis had done so much to foment were re-ignited in Eastern Europe.

But the end of the World War II was also a time of vengeance and judicial reckoning. The newly-liberated countries of Europe punished all those they thought had been collaborators. Hundreds of thousands of Cossacks, Russians and Ukrainians who fought alongside the Germans were repatriated to face almost cer-

General George Marshall.

The Nuremberg trials: Nazi leaders listen to legal arguments.

tain death in Stalin's gulags. German PoWs were kept in Siberian camps, and the few thousand survivors were not finally released until 1955.

The Allied powers also began to bring traitors and war criminals to justice. William Joyce, who had broadcast from Germany as 'Lord Haw-Haw', was hanged for treason; his Japanese equivalent, 'Tokyo Rose', was sentenced to ten years in prison. More significantly, those responsible for the Holocaust were put through a legitimate judicial process. On 20 October 1945, 22 Nazis were indicted at the war crimes tribunal at Nuremberg. Evidence included over 100,000 captured documents. Goering escaped execution by committing suicide; the hanged included

A Japanese woman collects firewood in the ruins of her city.

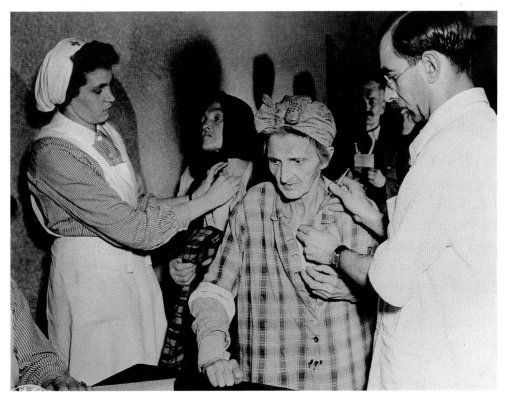

An old woman is inoculated at a displaced persons' camp, Austria.

General Tojo listens to his death sentence at the Tokyo war crime trials.

Ribbentrop and Keitel, their bodies cremated on the site of Dachau concentration camp. The West German government agreed to pay 3000 million German marks in compensation to the new state of Israel and another 450 million to Jewish organisations.

In Japan, foreign minister Togo was arrested for his part in the pre-war negotiations (Fumimaro, who had struggled to avoid war, committed suicide in December 1945). Generals Homma and Yamashita, responsible for the Bataan Death March and the destruction of Manila, were executed by firing squad in 1946. Soldiers responsible for the murder or torture of prisoners were tried and sentenced in Tokyo. For his role as a warmonger, Tojo was executed in 1948 – the only Axis head of state to receive a death sentence from the Allies.

Prosecutors at the Nuremberg and Tokyo trials relied not only on new legal principles such as 'crimes against humanity': they also used photographs and newsreels as the irrefutable evidence of genocide. Confronted by these often terrible images, some of the accused shut their eyes or turned away their faces. Though war and war crimes may always be with us, so will the means to document their barbarity, to shame and convict the perpetrators, and to provide a chastening record for the future.

Index

Picture acknowledgements

The publisher would like to thank the following photographic organisations for their contributions:
US National Archives, Washington DC
US Library of Congress, Washington DC
US Navy Photographic Division, Washington DC
US Airforce Photographic Division, Washington DC
US Marine Corps, Washington DC
Imperial War Museum, London
Robert Hunt Library, London
TRH Pictures, London
Polish Underground Movement, London
Polish Institute and Sikorsky Museum, London
London Fire Brigade, London
Museum of London
RAF Museum, London
J Baker Collection, Sussex, England
Biggin Hill Museum, Biggin Hill, England
Roger-Viollet, Paris
Renault Photographic Archive, Paris
Statto Maggiore Italiana, Rome